AMERICAN GOVERNMENT

STUDENT ACTIVITIES

FOURTH EDITION

bju press®
Greenville, South Carolina

Note: The fact that materials produced by other publishers may be referenced in this volume does not constitute an endorsement of the content or theological position of materials produced by such publishers. Any references and ancillary materials are listed as an aid to the student or the teacher and in an attempt to maintain the accepted academic standards of the publishing industry.

AMERICAN GOVERNMENT Student Activities
Fourth Edition

Writer
Joseph Jarrell, MS, MA

Contributing Writers
John Seney, MA
Sarah Weaver, MEd, MA

Previous Edition Writers
Lynn Garland
Dennis Peterson, MS

Biblical Worldview
Brian Collins, PhD

Academic Oversight
Rachel Santopietro, MEd

Editor
Manda Kalagayan, MEd

Cover and Book Concept
Drew Fields

Cover and Book Design
Dan VanLeeuwen

Page Layout
Sarah Centers

Project Manager
Dan Berger

Permissions
Sharon Belknap
Sarah Gundlach
Elizabeth Walker

Consultant
Linda Abrams, MA

Photo Credits
front cover eurobanks/Shutterstock.com; **front matter** ablokhin/iStock/Getty Images Plus/Getty Images; **chs. 1–3** © iStock.com/AndreyKrav; **chs. 4–7** Library of Congress, DIG-highsm-15714; **chs. 8–9** © iStock.com/drnadig; **chs. 10–13** ZRyzner/Shutterstock.com; **chs. 14–15** stock_photo_world/Shutterstock.com; **chs. 16–18** Library of Congress, DIG-ds-11910; **back cover** Craig Oesterling/BJU Press/Campaign buttons courtesy of Joseph Jarrell

Text acknowledgments appear on-page with text selections.

© 2020 BJU Press
Greenville, South Carolina 29609

First Edition © 2004 BJU Press
Second Edition © 2014 BJU Press

Printed in the United States of America
All rights reserved

ISBN 978-1-62856-542-3

15 14 13 12 11 10 9 8 7 6 5 4 3 2 1

CONTENTS

UNIT I: AMERICA'S FOUNDATIONS
Chapter 1: The Only Sure Foundation
- Activity 1: An Election Sermon by Abraham Williams, 1762. ... 1
- Activity 2: A Lesson from Literature ... 3
- Activity 3: Psalm 72: God's Ideal for Government ... 5
- Activity 4: Obligations of the Government and the Governed ... 7
- Activity 5: Chapter Review ... 9

Chapter 2: Forms of Government
- Activity 1: Systems of Government ... 11
- Activity 2: The Rise of Tyranny in Ancient Greece ... 13
- Activity 3: Thucydides: Pericles's Description of Democracy in Athens ... 15
- Activity 4: Walter Williams: Democracy and Majority Rule ... 17
- Activity 5: Chapter Review ... 19

Chapter 3: Christianity, the Church, and Government
- Activity 1: Mayflower Compact, 1620 ... 21
- Activity 2: John Locke's Views Regarding Religious Toleration ... 23
- Activity 3: Jefferson and the "Wall of Separation" ... 25
- Activity 4: Chapter Review ... 27

UNIT II: THE CONSTITUTION
Chapter 4: Constitutional Beginnings
- Activity 1: Declaration and Resolves ... 29
- Activity 2: John Locke's Views Regarding Government ... 31
- Activity 3: The Constitution and Limited Government ... 33
- Activity 4: Patrick Henry, Anti-Federalist ... 35
- Activity 5: Chapter Review ... 37

Chapter 5: The United States Constitution
- Activity 1: Why Was the Constitution Written? ... 39
- Activity 2: Strict or Broad Constructionist? ... 41
- Activity 3: Popular Sovereignty ... 42
- Activity 4: Differing Viewpoints Regarding Judicial Review ... 43
- Activity 5: Chapter Review ... 45

Chapter 6: Federalism
- Activity 1: Federalism's Development ... 47
- Activity 2: Revenue Sharing ... 49
- Activity 3: A Brief History of American Federalism ... 51
- Activity 4: Chapter Review ... 53

Chapter 7: State and Local Government
- Activity 1: When There Is No Government ... 55
- Activity 2: Researching Your State and Local Governments ... 57
- Activity 3: Eminent Domain ... 61
- Activity 4: Chapter Review ... 63

UNIT III: THE LEGISLATIVE BRANCH
Chapter 8: The Structure of Congress
- Activity 1: Congress and Its Leaders ... 65
- Activity 2: Your Representative's and Senators' Committee Assignments ... 67
- Activity 3: A Bill Becomes Law ... 68
- Activity 4: Chapter Review ... 69

Chapter 9: The Powers of Congress
- Activity 1: War Powers Resolution ... 71
- Activity 2: Design a Stamp ... 73
- Activity 3: The Bible and Poverty ... 74
- Activity 4: Growing Reliance on Government Support ... 75
- Activity 5: Chapter Review ... 77

UNIT IV: THE EXECUTIVE BRANCH
Chapter 10: The Road to the White House
- Activity 1: Choosing Qualified Leaders ... 79
- Activity 2: A Brokered Convention: The Democratic National Convention, 1924 ... 81
- Activity 3: Presidential Debates ... 83
- Activity 4: The Disputed Election of 1876 ... 85
- Activity 5: Chapter Review ... 87

Chapter 11: America's Highest Office
- Activity 1: President vs. King ... 89
- Activity 2: The Proper Attitude Toward the Powers of the Presidency ... 91
- Activity 3: Comparing First Ladies ... 93
- Activity 4: John Nance Garner on the Vice Presidency ... 95
- Activity 5: Comparing Presidents ... 97
- Activity 6: Chapter Review ... 99

Chapter 12: The Federal Bureaucracy
- Activity 1: The Case for Bureaucracy ... 101
- Activity 2: The Cabinet ... 103
- Activity 3: Is Administrative Law Constitutional? ... 105
- Activity 4: Bureaucracy Cartoon ... 107
- Activity 5: Chapter Review ... 109

Chapter 13: Foreign Policy
- Activity 1: US Foreign Policy Goals ... 111
- Activity 2: Foreign Policy Development ... 113
- Activity 3: Two Views of American Involvement in Foreign Affairs ... 115
- Activity 4: Chapter Review ... 119

UNIT V: THE JUDICIAL BRANCH
Chapter 14: The Judiciary
- Activity 1: The Principles of Blackstone's *Commentaries* ... 121
- Activity 2: Criteria for Supreme Court Justices ... 123
- Activity 3: *Marbury v. Madison* (1803) ... 125
- Activity 4: The Originalist Perspective ... 127
- Activity 5: Chapter Review ... 129

Chapter 15: Civil Liberties, Civil Rights, and Civil Responsibilities
Activity 1: Freedom of the Press 131
Activity 2: First Amendment Freedoms. 133
Activity 3: The Second Amendment 134
Activity 4: The Duties of Citizenship. 135
Activity 5: Chapter Review. 137

UNIT VI: PARTY POLITICS
Chapter 16: The Party System
Activity 1: Party Functions. 139
Activity 2: Voter Turnout in Presidential Elections. . . 140
Activity 3: Washington's Farewell Address. 141
Activity 4: Third Parties in American Politics. 143
Activity 5: Chapter Review. 145

Chapter 17: Campaigns and Elections
Activity 1: Becoming a Candidate. 147
Activity 2: The Role of New Media in
              Political Campaigning. 149
Activity 3: State Election Laws. 151
Activity 4: Summarizing Recent Elections 152
Activity 5: Chapter Review. 153

Chapter 18: Public Policy and Politics
Activity 1: Today's Issues 155
Activity 2: Opinions About Public Opinion 157
Activity 3: Contacting Public Officials 159
Activity 4: Mass Media Cartoon 160
Activity 5: Chapter Review. 161

AMERICAN GOVERNMENT

Name _____

CHAPTER 1 • ACTIVITY 1

An Election Sermon by Abraham Williams, 1762

Abraham Williams, pastor of a Congregationalist church in Sandwich, near Boston, delivered an Election Day sermon regarding the general principles of government. Read the sermon excerpts and then answer the questions.

"As to the origin of civil Societies or Governments; the Author of our Being, has given Man a Nature fitted for, and disposed to Society. It was not good for Man at first to be *alone*; his Nature is social, having various Affections, Propensities and Passions, which respect Society, and cannot be indulged without a social Intercourse: The natural Principles of Benevolence, Compassion, Justice, and indeed most of our natural Affections, powerfully incite to, and plainly indicate, that Man was formed for Society. To a Man detached from all Society, many essential Parts of his Frame are useless—are troublesome: He is unable to supply himself with many Materials of Happiness, which require the Assistance and Concurrence of others: Most of the *Conveniencies* of Life require the *Concurrence* of several. . . .

All Men being naturally equal, as descended from a common Parent, enbued with like Faculties and Propensities, having originally equal Rights and Properties, . . . yet Men not being equally industrious and frugal, their Properties and Enjoyments would be unequal. This would tempt the idle and imprudent to seize what they had not laboured for; which must put the industrious and honest upon Methods of Self-Defence, and dispose them to unite in Societies for mutual Security, against the Assaults of rapacious Men, as well as voracious Animals. The social affections of human Nature, and the Desire of the many Conveniencies, not to be obtained or enjoyed, without the concurrence of others, probably, first induced Men to associate together: the *Envy, Ambition, Covetousness,* and *Sensuality,* so much prevailing in the *Depraved* Nature of Man, since the *Apostacy,* obliged them to enter into closer Connections, Combinations and Compacts, for mutual Protection and Assistance. . . .

The End and Design of civil Society and Government, from this View of its Origin, must be to secure the Rights and Properties of its Members, and promote their Welfare; or in the Apostle's words, *that Men may lead quiet and peaceable Lives in Godliness and Honesty. . . .*"

Charles S. Hyneman and Donald Lutz, eds., *American Political Writing During the Founding Era: 1760-1805*, vol. 1 (Indianapolis: Liberty Fund, 1983).

1. What does Williams say was God's reason for giving mankind a "Nature fitted for . . . Society"?
   _____
   _____

2. Why does he say that people must protect themselves from each other in a civil society?
   _____
   _____
   _____
   _____

3. What examples of human depravity does Williams say first induced people to join in civil society?
   _____

(continued on next page)

4. Summarize Williams's beliefs about human government in your own words. _____
_____
_____
_____
_____

5. Although the preceding excerpts do not address the topic, how might these principles be applied to a nation's foreign policy? _____
_____
_____
_____
_____

AMERICAN GOVERNMENT

Name _____

CHAPTER 1 • ACTIVITY 2

A Lesson from Literature

In the poem "Ozymandius," British romantic poet Percy Shelley offers a poignant commentary on the rise and fall of nations. Ozymandius is the Greek name for Pharaoh Rameses II, who ruled Egypt for almost sixty-seven years during the thirteenth century BC. His rule was characterized by unsurpassed splendor and mammoth building projects, such as the temples at Abu Simbel and various structures at Karnak. Rameses's mummified remains are now stored in a Cairo museum. Even as an unregenerate man, Shelley's illustrates in "Ozymandius" the vanity of accomplishing great works apart from God. The rulers of this world pass away, but God and His Word are forever (1 Peter 1:24–25).

Read the poem carefully, and then answer the questions that follow.

> I met a traveler from an antique land
> Who said: "Two vast and trunkless legs of stone
> Stand in the desert. Near them, on the sand,
> Half sunk, a shattered visage lies, whose frown,
> And wrinkled lip, and sneer of cold command,   5
> Tell that its sculptor well those passions read
> Which yet survive, stamped on these lifeless things,
> The hand that mocked them, and the heart that fed;
> And on the pedestal these words appear:
> 'My name is Ozymandias, king of kings: 10
> Look on my works, ye mighty, and despair!'
> Nothing beside remains. Round the decay
> Of that colossal wreck, boundless and bare
> The lone and level sands stretch far away."

1. Why is the boast of Ozymandius as inscribed on the pedestal (see lines 10–11) ironic? _____
   _____
   _____
   _____

2. Name some other dictators from history who held similar visions of grandeur and pride only to have them dashed to pieces. _____
   _____
   _____
   _____

3. What biblical lessons can individuals take from this poem and the other examples from history?
   _____
   _____
   _____

AMERICAN GOVERNMENT

Name _____

CHAPTER 1 • ACTIVITY 3

Psalm 72: God's Ideal for Government

King David wrote this psalm for his son Solomon. As the content of the psalm makes clear, this psalm looks far beyond the rule of Solomon to the rule of the messianic King. But it has lessons for all rulers about God's ideal for government. [Note: "Judgment" could also be translated "justice."]

Read the psalm and answer the following questions.

A psalm for Solomon

Give the king thy judgments, O God,
and thy righteousness unto the king's son.
He shall judge thy people with righteousness,
and thy poor with judgment.

The mountains shall bring peace to the people,
and the little hills, by righteousness.
He shall judge the poor of the people,
he shall save the children of the needy,
and shall break in pieces the oppressor.
They shall fear thee as long as the sun and moon endure,
throughout all generations.
He shall come down like rain upon the mown grass:
as showers that water the earth.
In his days shall the righteous flourish;
and abundance of peace so long as the moon endureth.
He shall have dominion also from sea to sea,
and from the river unto the ends of the earth.
They that dwell in the wilderness shall bow before him;
and his enemies shall lick the dust.
The kings of Tarshish and of the isles shall bring presents:
the kings of Sheba and Seba shall offer gifts.
Yea, all kings shall fall down before him:
all nations shall serve him.

For he shall deliver the needy when he crieth;
the poor also, and him that hath no helper.
He shall spare the poor and needy,
and shall save the souls of the needy.
He shall redeem their soul from deceit and violence:
and precious shall their blood be in his sight.

And he shall live, and to him shall be given of the gold of Sheba:
prayer also shall be made for him continually;
and daily shall he be praised.
There shall be an handful of corn in the earth upon the top of the mountains;
the fruit thereof shall shake like Lebanon:
and they of the city shall flourish like grass of the earth.

(continued on next page)

His name shall endure for ever:
his name shall be continued as long as the sun:
and men shall be blessed in him:
all nations shall call him blessed.

Blessed be the LORD God,
the God of Israel, who only doeth wondrous things.
And blessed be his glorious name for ever:
and let the whole earth be filled with his glory;
Amen, and Amen.

The prayers of David the son of Jesse are ended.

1. List three things in this psalm that clearly apply only to the Messiah (and not to other earthly rulers). For example: He shall be feared as long as the sun and moon endure throughout all generations.
   _____
   _____
   _____
   _____

2. List three obligations for all governments from this passage. For example: He [the ruler] shall judge people with righteousness (in other words, he will judge righteously). _____
   _____
   _____
   _____

3. What does the following imagery reveal about the effect of righteous rule: "He shall come down like rain upon the mown grass. In his days shall the righteous flourish"; "and shall break in pieces the oppressor . . . and his enemies shall lick the dust"? _____
   _____
   _____
   _____

4. Write a prayer based on the psalm that you can pray during this course for the officials who govern you.
   _____
   _____
   _____
   _____
   _____

AMERICAN GOVERNMENT

Name _____

CHAPTER 1 • ACTIVITY 4

Obligations of the Government and the Governed

Read the following Scripture passages that relate to the responsibilities of the government and the governed, and then answer the questions that follow.

Deuteronomy 1:16–17

1. What was the primary responsibility of Israel's judges? _____
   _____

2. What were they not to take into account when they judged? _____
   _____
   _____

Proverbs 29:2, 4, 7, 12

3. Contrast the righteous ruler and the wicked (or unwise) ruler in these verses. _____
   _____
   _____
   _____

Matthew 22:16–21

4. Emperors, or Caesars, headed the Roman government. They were often unrighteous. What did Jesus say about paying taxes to such a government? _____
   _____

5. If people are to render to Caesar the things that bear his image, what is to be rendered to God (see Genesis 1:26–27)? _____
   _____

Acts 4:13–20, 27–29

6. How should the Christian respond if a government mandate contradicts one or more of God's commands?
   _____

Titus 3:1–2

7. What responsibilities toward government does Paul give Christians in this passage? _____
   _____
   _____

(continued on next page)

Acts 16:16–39

8. How did the officials in this passage violate Roman law? _____
_____

9. How had Paul and Silas responded to this unlawful situation (v. 25, 31–32)? _____
_____
_____

10. How did Paul make the government officials accountable for their actions? _____
_____
_____

Acts 23:1–5 and Exodus 22:28

11. What was Paul's response to being struck? _____
_____
_____

12. How did Paul change his response when he learned who had given the order? _____
_____
_____
_____

Romans 13:1–7; 1 Peter 2:13–17

13. What is every person's responsibility toward governing authorities? _____
_____
_____

14. Why does God command this response to governing authorities? _____
_____
_____
_____
_____

15. What are the responsibilities of government according to this passage? _____
_____
_____
_____

AMERICAN GOVERNMENT

Name _____

CHAPTER 2 • ACTIVITY 1

Systems of Government

Define the four major government systems below. For each, list a nation (mentioned in the textbook) that has or has had that system.

1. Popular government—_____
   _____

2. Dictatorship—_____
   _____

3. Anarchy—_____
   _____

4. Monarchy—_____
   _____

Identify whether each of the following statements is describing a unitary, federal, or confederate government.

_____ 5. The national government has few powers.

_____ 6. The government's power resides in the central government.

_____ 7. The Articles of Confederation established this type of government in early American history.

_____ 8. A nation's power is divided between national and regional governments.

_____ 9. Local units are created by the central government to help administer governments.

_____ 10. This government guards against tyranny through the separation of its powers.

_____ 11. The European Union is an example of this government type.

_____ 12. Israel and Japan are examples of this government type.

_____ 13. This type of government works well in large countries made up of people with different needs and goals.

_____ 14. Brazil and India are examples of this government type.

(continued on next page)

11

Using outside resources, identify whether the following countries elect their chief executives through a presidential or a parliamentary system.

_____ 15. Bolivia

_____ 16. Czech Republic

_____ 17. Fiji

_____ 18. United Kingdom

_____ 19. Mexico

_____ 20. Ecuador

_____ 21. Egypt

_____ 22. Japan

_____ 23. Uzbekistan

_____ 24. Zimbabwe

AMERICAN GOVERNMENT

CHAPTER 2 • ACTIVITY 2

Name _____

The Rise of Tyranny in Ancient Greece

Read the following excerpts from the writings of two ancient historians—Herodotus and Plutarch. Then answer the questions.

Herodotus Describes Tyranny Coming to Corinth

. . . Sosicles the Corinthian . . . exclaimed—"[S]ince you, Lacedaemonians [people from the area around the Greek city-state of Sparta], propose to put down free governments in the cities of Greece, and to set up tyrannies in their room [stead]. There is nothing in the whole world so unjust, nothing so bloody, as a tyranny. . . . If you knew what tyranny was as well as ourselves, you would be better advised than you now are in regard to it. The government at Corinth was once an oligarchy—a single race, called Bacchiadae, who intermarried only among themselves, held the management of affairs. . . . Aetion's [one of the Bacchiadae] son grew up, and, in remembrance of the danger from which he had excaped, was named Cypselus.
. . . [He] became master of Corinth. Having thus got the tyranny, he showed himself a harsh ruler—many of the Corinthians he drove into banishment, many he deprived of his fortunes, and a still greater number of their lives. His reign lasted thirty years, and was prosperous to its close; insomuch that he left the government to Periander, his son. . . . Where Cypselus had spared any, and had neither put them to death nor banished them, Periander completed what his father had left unfinished."

Herodotus, *The Histories*. Public domain.

1. What type of government did the Lacedaemonians propose to substitute for the free governments they were planning to defeat? _____

2. What form of government did Corinth have before it fell under the rule of tyranny? _____

3. What did Cypselus do once he became tyrant over Corinth? _____
_____

4. What kind of ruler was Cypselus's son, Periander? _____
_____

(continued on next page)

Plutarch Describes Tyranny Coming to Athens

But the people of Athens were again divided into factions while Solon [an Athenian ruler in the 6th century BC] was away. The Plain-men [plains people] were headed by Lycurgus; the Shore-men [seaside people] by Megacles . . . , and the Hill-men [hill people] by Peisistratus. Among the last was the multitude of Thetes, who were the bitter enemies of the rich. As a consequence . . . all were already expecting a revolution and desirous of a different form of government . . . each party thinking to be bettered by the change, and to get the entire mastery of its opponents. Such was the state of affairs when Solon returned to Athens. He was revered and honoured by all, but owing to his years he no longer had the strength or the ardour to speak and act in public as before. He did, however, confer privately with the chiefs of the opposing factions, endeavouring to reconcile and harmonize them, and Peisistratus seemed to pay him more heed than the others. For Peisistratus had an insinuating and agreeable quality in his address, he was ready to help the poor, and was reasonable and moderate in his enmities [hostilities; bitterness]. . . . He was thought to be a cautious and order-loving man, one that prized equality above all things. . . . [H]e completely deceived most people. . . .

Now when Peisistratus, after inflicting a wound upon himself, came into the market-place riding in a chariot, and tried to exasperate the populace with the charge that his enemies had plotted against his life on account of his political opinions, . . . many of them greeted the charge with angry cries. . . . After this the multitude was ready to fight for Peisistratus, and a general assembly of the people was held. Here Ariston made a motion that Peisistratus be allowed a body-guard of fifty club-bearers, but Solon formally opposed it. . . . [W]hen he [Solon] saw that the poor were tumultuously bent on gratifying Peisistratus, . . . he left the assembly. . . . So the people passed the decree, and then held Peisistratus to no strict account of the number of his club-bearers, but suffered him to keep and lead about in public as many as he wished, until at last he seized the acropolis [the hilltop in Athens where the most important buildings were located; the center of the city-state].

Plutarch, *The Lives: Solon*. Public domain.

5. What resulted when Solon was away from Athens? _____

6. How did the people view Solon? _____

7. What qualities won Peisistratus the confidence of the people when Solon proved unable to rule because of age? _____

8. What did Peisistratus further do to gain his support from the people? _____

9. Who earnestly but unsuccessfully opposed this decision? _____

10. What did Peisistratus seize? _____

AMERICAN GOVERNMENT

Name _____

CHAPTER 2 • ACTIVITY 3

Thucydides: Pericles's Description of Democracy in Athens

The ancient historian Thucydides recorded a funeral oration by the great Athenian leader Pericles after one of the early battles of the Peloponnesian War. In it, Pericles described the democracy of Athens. Read the following excerpts and answer the questions.

We live under a form of government which does not emulate [imitate] the institutions of our neighbours; on the contrary, we are ourselves a model which some follow. . . . It is true that our government is called a democracy, because its administration is in the hands, not of the few, but of the many; yet while as regards the law all men are on an equality for the settlement of their private disputes . . . not because he belongs to a particular class, but because of personal merits; nor, again, on the ground of poverty is a man barred from a public career by obscurity of rank if he but has it in him to do the state a service. And not only in our public life are we liberal, but also as regards our freedom from suspicion of one another in the pursuits of every-day life; for we do not feel resentment at our neighbour if he does as he likes, nor yet do we put on sour looks which, though harmless, are painful to behold. But while we thus avoid giving offence in our private intercourse, in our public life we are restrained from lawlessness chiefly through reverent fear, for we render obedience to those in authority and to the laws, and especially to those laws which are ordained for the succour of the oppressed and those which, though unwritten, bring upon the transgressor a disgrace which all men recognize.

Moreover, we have provided for the spirit many relaxations from toil: we have games and sacrifices regularly throughout the year and homes fitted out with good taste and elegance; and the delight we each day find in these things drives away sadness. And our city is so great that all the products of all the earth flow in upon us, and ours is the happy lot to gather in the good fruits of our own soil. . . .

We are also superior to our opponents in our system of training for warfare, and this in the following respects. In the first place, we throw our city open to all the world and we never by exclusion acts debar any one from learning or seeing anything which an enemy might profit by observing if it were not kept from his sight; for we place our dependence, not so much upon prearranged devices to deceive, as upon the courage which springs from our own souls when we are called to action. And again, in the matter of education, whereas they from early childhood by a laborious discipline make pursuit of manly courage, we with our unrestricted mode of life are none the less ready to meet any equality of hazard. . . .

1. What was the government of Athens called? _____

2. Why was it called this? _____

3. What did Athens provide so that people could relax and feel content? _____

4. What was the Athenian policy concerning visitors to the city-state? What, if any, were the dangers of this policy? _____

(continued on next page)

For we are lovers of beauty yet with no extravagance and lovers of wisdom yet without weakness. Wealth we employ rather as an opportunity for action than as a subject for boasting; and with us it is not a shame for a man to acknowledge poverty, but the greater shame is for him not to do his best to avoid it. And you will find united in the same persons an interest at once in private and in public affairs, and in others of us who give attention chiefly to business, you will find no lack of insight into political matters. For we alone regard the man who takes no part in public affairs, not as one who minds his own business, but as good for nothing; and we Athenians decide public questions for ourselves or at least endeavour to arrive at a sound understanding of them, in the belief that it is not debate that is a hindrance to action, but rather not to be instructed by debate before the time comes for action. . . .

And, finally, we alone confer our benefits without fear of consequences, not upon a calculation of the advantage we shall gain, but with confidence in the spirit of liberality which actuates us.

. . . [I]t seems to me, each individual amongst us could in his own person, with the utmost grace and versatility, prove himself self-sufficient in the most varied forms of activity. And that this is no mere boast inspired by the occasion, but actual truth, is attested by the very power of our city, a power which we have acquired in consequence of these qualities. For Athens alone among her contemporaries, when put to the test, is superior to the report of her, and she alone neither affords to the enemy who comes against her cause for irritation at the character of the foe by whom he is defeated, nor to her subject cause for complaint that his masters are unworthy. Many are the proofs which we have given of our power and assuredly it does not lack witnesses, and therefore we shall be the wonder not only of the men of to-day but of after times. . . .

Charles Forster Smith, trans., *Thucydides*, vol. 2 (Cambridge: Harvard University Press, 1962).

5. What does Pericles say it is not a shame to acknowledge? What is a greater shame? _____

6. How did the Athenians view someone who did not participate in public affairs (political matters)? _____

7. How did Athenians view debate about public issues? _____

8. What does the closing sentence of the excerpt mean? _____

AMERICAN GOVERNMENT

CHAPTER 2 • ACTIVITY 4

Walter Williams: Democracy and Majority Rule

Read this essay by economist and political scientist Walter Williams. Then choose and complete one of the two writing (or speaking) activities that follow.

Democracy and majority rule give an aura of legitimacy to acts that would otherwise be deemed tyranny. Think about it. How many decisions in our day-to-day lives would we like to be made through majority rule or the democratic process? How about the decision whether you should watch a football game on television or "Law & Order"? What about whether you drive a Chevrolet or a Ford, or whether your Easter dinner is turkey or ham? Were such decisions made in the political arena, most of us would deem it tyranny. Why isn't it also tyranny for the democratic process to mandate what type of light bulbs we use, how many gallons of water to flush toilets or whether money should be taken out of our paycheck for retirement?

The founders of our nation held a deep abhorrence for democracy and majority rule. In Federalist Paper No. 10, James Madison wrote: "Measures are too often decided, not according to the rules of justice and the rights of the minor party, but by the superior force of an interested and overbearing majority." John Adams predicted: "Remember, democracy never lasts long. It soon wastes, exhausts, and murders itself. There was never a democracy yet that did not commit suicide." Our founders intended for us to have a republican form of limited government where the protection of individual God-given rights was the primary job of government.

Alert to the dangers of majoritarian tyranny, the Constitution's framers inserted several anti-majority rules. One such rule is that election of the president is not decided by a majority vote but instead by the Electoral College. Nine states have more than 50% of the US population. If a simple majority were the rule, conceivably these nine states could determine the presidency. Fortunately they can't, since they have only 225 Electoral College votes when 270 of the 538 total are needed. Were it not for the Electoral College, which some politicians say is antiquated and would like to do away with, presidential candidates could safely ignore the less-populous states.

Part of the reason our founders created two houses of Congress was to have another obstacle to majority rule. Fifty-one senators can block the designs of 435 representatives and 49 senators. The Constitution gives the president a veto to weaken the power of 535 members of both houses of Congress. It takes two-thirds of both houses of Congress to override a presidential veto.

To change the constitution requires not a majority but a two-thirds vote of both Houses to propose an amendment, and to be enacted requires ratification by three-fourths of state legislatures. The Constitution's Article V empowers two-thirds of state legislatures to call for a constitutional convention to propose amendments that become law when ratified by three-fourths of state legislatures. . . .

In addition to an abhorrence of democracy, and the recognition that government posed the gravest threat to liberty, our founders harbored a deep distrust and suspicion of Congress. This suspicion and distrust is exemplified by the phraseology used throughout the Constitution, particularly our Bill of Rights, containing phrases such as Congress shall not: abridge, infringe, deny, disparage or violate. Today's Americans think Congress has the constitutional authority to do anything upon which they can get a majority vote. We think whether a particular measure is a good idea or bad idea should determine passage as opposed to whether that measure lies within the enumerated powers granted Congress by the Constitution.

Unfortunately for the future of our nation, Congress has successfully exploited American constitutional ignorance or contempt.

© 2009 Creators Syndicate, Inc. By permission of Walter E. Williams and Creators Syndicate, Inc.

(continued on next page)

1. Using this essay as a foundation, write an essay (or prepare an oral presentation) titled "The Tyranny of Majority Rule." Use outside sources to support your points. Read (or deliver) your essay or presentation to your class.

2. Write an essay (or prepare an oral presentation) titled "Dangers to Our Constitution." Emphasize the ignorance of the average citizen (and even some elected officials) about our Constitution. Support your points using items from current events. Then read (or deliver) your essay or presentation to your class.

AMERICAN GOVERNMENT

Name _____

CHAPTER 3 • ACTIVITY 1

Mayflower Compact, 1620

The Mayflower Compact was the first document establishing a form of government in colonial America. Read it and answer the questions that follow.

   In the name of God, Amen. We, whose names are underwritten, the loyal subjects of our dread Sovereign Lord, *King James*, by the grace of God, of *Great Britain, France* and *Ireland* king, *defender of the faith, etc.* Having undertaken for the glory of God, and advancement of the Christian faith, and honour of our king and country, a voyage to plant the first colony in the Northern parts of *Virginia*; do by these presents solemnly and mutually, in the presence of God and one of another, covenant and combine ourselves together into a civil body politick, for our better ordering and preservation, and furtherance of the ends aforesaid: and by virtue hereof to enact, constitute, and frame, such just and equal laws, ordinances, acts, constitutions and offices, from time to time, as shall be thought most meet and convenient for the general good of the Colony; unto which we promise all due submission and obedience. In witness whereof we have hereunder subscribed our names at *Cape-Cod* the eleventh of *November*, in the reign of our sovereign lord, *King James,* of *England, France* and *Ireland*, the eighteenth, and of *Scotland* the fifty-fourth, *Anno Domini*, 1620.

1. Who was the British king at the time this document was written? _____

2. The document lists three reasons the Pilgrims had taken the voyage to the New World. What were those?
   _____
   _____

For questions 3–6, explain the meaning of the following phrases from the Mayflower Compact.

3. "covenant and combine ourselves together into a civil body politick" _____
   _____

4. "for our better ordering and preservation" _____
   _____

5. "by virtue hereof to enact, constitute, and frame such just and equal laws, ordinances, acts, constitutions, and offices" _____
   _____

6. "unto which we promise all due submission and obedience" _____
   _____

7. What was the month, day, and year this document was signed? _____

AMERICAN GOVERNMENT

Name _____

CHAPTER 3 • ACTIVITY 2

John Locke's Views Regarding Religious Toleration

In 1689, the philosopher John Locke wrote *A Letter Concerning Toleration*. In it, he gave his ideas about the relationship between government and the church. He cited how he thought the two should work with each other and argued for religious toleration.

Excerpts from that letter, which spans more than forty pages, are provided below. You will note his frequent use of the word "magistrate" when referring to a government or church official.

Read the excerpts and answer the questions.

By this we see what difference there is between the church and the commonwealth [the government]. Whatsoever is lawful in the commonwealth, cannot be prohibited by the magistrate in the church.

1. Restate what Locke is writing here. _____
_____

But those things that are prejudicial [detrimental] to the common weal [good] of a people in their ordinary use, and are therefore forbidden by laws, those things ought not to be permitted to churches in their sacred rites. [Earlier Locke gave the example of religions that practice human sacrifice.] . . . The [government] magistrate ought always to be very careful, that he do[es] not misuse his authority, to the oppression of any church, under pretense of public good.

2. Explain what Locke is saying. _____
_____
_____
_____

It may be said, "What if a church be idolatrous [Locke is referring to a church that does not follow true Christian teachings], is that also to be tolerated by the [government] magistrate?" In answer, I ask, What power can be given to the magistrate for the suppression of an idolatrous church, which may not, in time and place, be made use of to the ruin of an orthodox one?

3. What is Locke saying? _____
_____
_____

(continued on next page)

© 2020 BJU Press. Reproduction prohibited.

23

These things being thus explained, it is easy to understand to what end the legislative power ought to be directed . . . and that is the temporal good and outward prosperity of the society. . . . But some may ask, What if the [government] magistrate should enjoin [order] any thing by his authority that appears unlawful to the conscience of a private person? I answer, That if government be faithfully administered, and the counsels of the magistrate be indeed directed to the public good, this will seldom happen. But if perhaps it do so fall out; I say, that such a private person is to abstain from the action that he judges unlawful, and he is to undergo the punishment, which it is not unlawful for him to bear.

4. What does Locke say is the goal of government [the legislative power]? _____

5. Locke had been asked what should be done if a government official decrees something that violates the conscience of an individual. What is his answer? _____

6. Why do you think many people today would argue that Locke's view (that the government would rarely order something to be done that would violate a person's conscience) is unrealistic? _____

But to come to particulars. I say, first, No opinions contrary to human society, or to those moral rules which are necessary to the preservation of civil society, are to be tolerated by the [government] magistrate. But of these, indeed examples in any church are rare. For no sect can easily arrive to such a degree of madness, as that it should think fit to teach, for doctrines of religion, such things as manifestly undermine the foundations of society, and are therefore condemned by the judgment of all mankind: because their own interest, peace, refutation, every thing, would be thereby endangered.

7. In your own words, what does Locke say a government official should not tolerate? _____

8. According to Locke, how often would a church teach something that government should not tolerate? Why? Do you think that Locke is accurate? _____

Lastly, Those are not at all to be tolerated who deny the being of a God. Promises, covenants, and oaths, which are the bonds of human society, can have no hold upon an atheist. The taking away of God, though but even in thought, dissolves all.

Locke, John. *A Letter Concerning Toleration*. Huddersfield, J. Brook, 1796.

9. In this letter, Locke argued that religious toleration is good and that government and churches should get along with each other. However, he now mentions a group that should not be tolerated. Explain. _____

AMERICAN GOVERNMENT

CHAPTER 3 • ACTIVITY 3

Jefferson and the "Wall of Separation"

In October 1801 the Danbury Baptist Association wrote a letter to President Thomas Jefferson, who had become president less than a year earlier. This Connecticut group consisted of more than twenty-five churches. They were concerned because Congregationalism was the established church in their state. Although the First Amendment prohibited Congress from establishing an official church, individual states could still do so. As a religious minority, they were concerned about the need for religious freedom in the relatively young nation.

Jefferson replied on New Year's Day of 1802, assuring them that he understood their concerns and declaring "a wall of separation between Church and State" existed. This phrase has been much misunderstood, misused, and abused over the generations.

Read the excerpts from the two letters and answer the questions.

Letter from the Danbury Baptists to Thomas Jefferson, October 7, 1801

Sir,

Among the many millions in America and Europe who rejoice in your election to office, we embrace the first opportunity which we have enjoyed in our collective capacity, since your inauguration, to express our great satisfaction in your appointment to the Chief Magistracy in the United States. . . .

Our sentiments are uniformly on the side of religious liberty: that Religion is at all times and places a matter between God and individuals, that no man ought to suffer in name, person, or effects on account of his religious opinions, [and] that the legitimate power of civil government extends no further than to punish the man who works ill to his neighbor. But sir, our constitution of government is not specific. . . . What religious privileges we enjoy (as a minor part of the State) we enjoy as favors granted, and not as inalienable rights. . . .

Sir, we are sensible that the President of the United States is not the National Legislator and also sensible that the national government cannot destroy the laws of each State, but our hopes are strong that the sentiments of our beloved President, which have had such genial [cordial] effect already, like the radiant beams of the sun, will shine and prevail through all these States—and all the world—until hierarchy and tyranny be destroyed from the earth. Sir, when we reflect on your past services, and see a glow of philanthropy and goodwill shining forth in a course of more than thirty years, we have reason to believe that America's God has raised you up to fill the Chair of State out of that goodwill which he bears to the millions which you preside over. May God strengthen you for the arduous task which providence and the voice of the people have called you—to sustain and support you and your Administration against all the predetermined opposition of those who wish to rise to wealth and importance on the poverty and subjection of the people.

And may the Lord preserve you safe from every evil and bring you at last to his Heavenly Kingdom through Jesus Christ our Glorious Mediator.

1. According to the Danbury Baptists, what is the limit of government authority? _____
   _____

2. What did the Danbury Baptists say about the Constitution, and why did they believe this? _____
   _____
   _____

(continued on next page)

President Jefferson's Reply

January 1, 1802

Gentlemen,—The affectionate sentiments of esteem and approbation [support] which you are so good as to express towards me, on behalf of the Danbury Baptist Association, give me the highest satisfaction. My duties dictate a faithful and zealous pursuit of the interests of my constituents, and in proportion as they are persuaded of my fidelity to those duties, the discharge of them becomes more and more pleasing.

Believing with you that religion is a matter which lies solely between man and his God, that he owes account to none other for his faith or his worship, . . . I contemplate with sovereign reverence that act of the whole American people which declared that their legislature [Congress] would "make no law respecting an establishment of religion, or prohibiting the free exercise thereof," [note: here Jefferson is quoting directly from the First Amendment to the Constitution] thus building a wall of separation between Church and State. Adhering to this expression of the supreme will of the nation in behalf of the rights of conscience, I shall see with sincere satisfaction the progress of those sentiments which tend to restore to man all his natural rights. . . .

I reciprocate your kind prayers for the protection and blessing of the common Father and Creator of man, and tender you for yourselves and your religious association, assurances of my high respect and esteem.

Th Jefferson

3. What two things did Jefferson believe about religion? _____

4. What does the First Amendment to the Constitution say about Congress? _____

5. What did Jefferson say the First Amendment built? _____

6. Carefully read the excerpt from the First Amendment. Do you think Jefferson's reference to a wall is an accurate portrayal of what is stated there? Why? _____

AMERICAN GOVERNMENT

Name _____

CHAPTER 4 • ACTIVITY 1

Declaration and Resolves

In 1774, members of the First Continental Congress, in defense of their rights as British subjects, compiled a list of grievances to be sent to King George III. Read the following excerpts from that document, the Declaration and Resolves. Answer the questions that follow.

    Whereas, since the close of the last war [the French and Indian War that ended in 1763], the British parliament, claiming a power, of right, to bind the people of America by statutes in all cases whatsoever, hath, in some acts, expressly imposed taxes on them . . . for the purpose of raising a revenue, hath imposed rates and duties payable in these colonies, established a board of commissioners, with unconstitutional powers, and extended the jurisdiction of courts of admiralty [shipping, trading], not only for collecting the said duties, but for the trial of causes merely arising within the body of a country:

    And whereas, in consequence of other statutes, judges . . . have been made dependent on the crown [king] alone for their salaries, and standing armies kept in times of peace:

    And whereas it has lately been resolved in parliament, that by force of a statute, made in the thirty-fifth year of the reign of King Henry the Eighth [in other words, a law that was more than two centuries old], colonists may be transported to England, and tried there upon accusations for treasons . . . or concealments of treasons committed in the colonies.

1. When did the Continental Congress say that the British Parliament had begun to "bind the people of America by statutes"? _____

2. For what purpose did Parliament impose rates and duties? _____

3. What did Parliament establish that used unconstitutional powers? _____

4. How was the jurisdiction of the courts of admiralty extended? _____

5. How had Parliament changed the method of paying judges? Why do you think this could prove to be a problem? _____

6. Why do you think keeping a standing army during times of peace was a grievance? _____

7. What statute had Parliament enforced that was more than two hundred years old? Why do you think this was a grievance? _____

8. For what crimes could colonists be tried in England? _____

(continued on next page)

And whereas, assemblies have been frequently dissolved, contrary to the rights of the people, when they attempted to deliberate on grievances, and their dutiful, humble, loyal, and reasonable petitions to the crown for redress, have been repeatedly treated with contempt, by his Majesty's ministers of state:

The good people of the several colonies of New-Hampshire, Massachusetts-Bay, Rhode Island and Providence Plantations, Connecticut, New-York, New-Jersey, Pennsylvania, Newcastle, Kent, and Sussex on Delaware, Maryland, Virginia, North-Carolina and South-Carolina, justly alarmed at these arbitrary proceedings of parliament and administration, have severally elected, constituted, and appointed deputies to meet, and sit in general Congress, in the city of Philadelphia, in order to obtain such establishment, as that their religion, laws, and liberties, may not be subverted [taken away]. . . .

9. How were the colonists treated when they expressed their grievances? _____
_____
_____

10. Why had the colonies sent delegates (deputies) to Philadelphia? _____
_____

Below is a partial list of those who signed the Declaration and Resolves. Choose an individual and briefly research his life. Then write a paragraph regarding the most interesting facts about him.

Colony	Signers
New Hampshire	John Sullivan and Nathaniel Folsom
Massachusetts	Thomas Cushing and Robert Treat Paine
Rhode Island	Stephen Hopkins and Samuel Ward
Connecticut	Eliphalet Dyer and Roger Sherman
New York	John Alsop and Isaac Low
Pennsylvania	John Morton and Edward Biddle
New Jersey	Stephen Crane and William Livingston
Delaware	Caesar Rodney and Thomas McKeane
Maryland	William Pace and Samuel Chase
Virginia	Richard Henry Lee and Benjamin Harrison
North Carolina	Joseph Hawes and Richard Caswell
South Carolina	Henry Middleton and Thomas Lynch

AMERICAN GOVERNMENT

CHAPTER 4 • ACTIVITY 2

John Locke's Views Regarding Government

In 1689, English philosopher John Locke wrote *Two Treatises of Government*. This was shortly after the Glorious Revolution in his country. In that event, Parliament forced King James II to abdicate (give up his throne). Locke believed that event was justified and argued in his *Two Treatises of Government* that people have the right, under certain circumstances, to rebel against their government.

Read the excerpts and answer the questions.

The reasons why men enter into society [and form a government] is the preservation of their property; and the end while they choose and authorize a legislative [lawmaking body] is that there may be laws made, and rules set, as guards and fences to the properties of all the society, to limit the power, and moderate the dominion of every part and member of the society.

1. Restate, in your own words, what Locke is stating above. _____

For since it can never be supposed to be the will of the society that the legislative should have a power to destroy that which every one designs to secure by entering into society, and for which the people submitted themselves to legislators of their own making; whenever the legislators endeavour to take away and destroy the property of the people, or to reduce them to slavery under arbitrary power, they put themselves into a state of war with the people, who are thereupon absolved from any farther obedience, and are left to the common refuge which God hath provided for all men against force and violence.

2. Locke identifies two times in which a government would be at war with its own people. What are those?

Whensoever, therefore, the legislative shall transgress this fundamental rule of society, and either by ambition, fear, folly, or corruption, endeavour to grasp themselves, or put into the hands of any other, an absolute power over the lives, liberties, and estates of the people; by this breach of trust they forfeit the power the people had put into their hands for quite contrary ends, and it devolves to the people, who have a right to resume their original liberty, and by the establishment of a new legislative (such as they shall think fit), provide for their own safety and security, which is the end for which they are in society.

3. What are some reasons government leaders might try to gain too much power (rather than complete the tasks for which government was formed)? _____

4. What do people have the right to do when government fails to fulfill its purposes? _____

(continued on next page)

[S]uch revolutions [should] happen not upon every little mismanagement in public affairs. Great mistakes in the ruling part, many wrong and inconvenient laws, and all the slips of human frailty will be borne by the people without mutiny or murmur. But if a long train of abuses, prevarications [deceitfulness], and artifices [scheming], all tending the same way, make the design visible to the people, and they cannot but feel what they lie under, and see whither they are going, it is not to be wondered that they should then rouse themselves, and endeavour to put the rule into such hands which may secure to them the ends for which government was at first erected. . . .

5. Describe the wrongs people should expect and endure from the government. _____
_____
_____

6. According to Locke when are people justified in rebelling against their government? _____
_____
_____

The end [purpose] of government is the good of mankind; and which is best for mankind, that the people should be always exposed to the boundless will of tyranny or that the rulers should be sometimes liable to be opposed [by the people] when they grow exorbitant [unreasonable] in the use of their power, and employ it for the destruction, and not the preservation, of the properties of their people?

John Locke, *Two Treatises of Government*, London: Routledge, 1884. 306–7, 309, 311.

7. What is the purpose of government? _____
_____

8. Summarize Locke's argument in this excerpt. _____
_____
_____
_____
_____

AMERICAN GOVERNMENT

Name _____

CHAPTER 4 • ACTIVITY 3

The Constitution and Limited Government

Read the following essay about the Constitution and limited government by historian Clarence Carson. Answer the accompanying questions.

As a document, there are some rather obvious things to be said about the Constitution. It is brief, concise, felicitously [appropriately] worded, yet surprisingly comprehensive in its description of and provisions for a government. Amendments were rare in the nineteenth century; there were only three between 1804 and 1913. Thus, it provided an example of stability as counterpoint to the argument that republics were unstable.

But, above all, the United States Constitution is informed by a few guiding principles. It established a republican form of government, which means that those who govern represent the electorate and are chosen directly or indirectly by them. The people do not govern directly but rather indirectly by those chosen to represent them or appointed by those so elected. Thus, while the majority rule holds sway, its impact is limited by a filtering process in a republic.

Second, the Constitution brought into being a federal system of government for the United States. What this means, essentially, is that the powers of government are divided between the general [national] government, on the one hand, and the states on the other. Each has a jurisdiction over the people within its bounds; each can act directly upon those in its jurisdiction, though what matters fall within the jurisdiction of the United States and of the states are usually different. This kind of federal structure was an American invention, invented in the course of the making of the Constitution.

There are other principles informing the Constitution, for example, the separation of powers, but there is one overarching principle which guides, makes necessary, and gives cogency [strength] to all the rest. That principle is limited government. Americans generally, and the Founders particularly, believed that if men are to be tolerably free governments must be limited. Now it was undoubtedly the case that the Constitutional Convention which met in 1787 assembled to provide for a more effective general government, one that would at least be adequate "to the exigencies [needs] of the Union," as was said. If they were bent on empowering and strengthening the general [national] government, how did this square with the principle of limited government? The most direct answer is that those who wanted a stronger and more effective government came to see that any plan to achieve that would only meet with general acceptance if it were more rigorously limited than those that preceded it.

1. How many constitutional amendments were adopted between 1804 and 1913? _____

2. Explain how a republican form of government functions. _____
   _____

3. What is a federal system of government? _____
   _____

4. Which principle in the Constitution does the author think is the most important one?
   _____

5. At the Constitutional Convention in 1787, the delegates wanted to strengthen the government. Why did they believe that a strong and more effective government would also have to be limited? _____
   _____

(continued on next page)

... Government must be limited to forestall tyranny. It must be limited so that it not trample on the rights of the people and usurp [take away] the powers of the states. The limitation of government was the counterbalance to the dangers of necessary government. ...

The distinctive thing about the United States Constitution is that it did about as thorough a job as could be done in limiting those who governed. The powers to be exercised were enumerated in the Constitution, and who was to exercise them listed. Not only are the branches of government separate from each other but they are independent of one another in their powers to negate government act. ...

... The first ten amendments are all precise limitations on government. The crowning one is the tenth which makes about as clear as can be that the United States government has only such powers as have been granted to it in the Constitution. It says, "The powers not delegated to the United States by the Constitution, nor prohibited by it to the States, are reserved to the States respectively, or to the people. ..."

In sum, the great and overarching principle informing the Constitution is that of limited government. ... However well the Constitution might be drawn and however carefully the government might be limited, the Founders doubted that liberty could prevail if the generality of governors and electorate became corrupt. And today, we must regretfully note that our Constitution no longer works as it was intended to do. It has been bent out of shape, particularly in the twentieth century, by those who would concentrate all power in the general [national] government and use that power to seduce and subdue the populace. Even so, the great principles are still there in the written Constitution, awaiting a sustained effort to limit government and free the people.

Clarence B. Carson, *The Foundations of American Constitutional Government*, 3rd Ed. (Irvington-on-Hudson, NY: The Foundation for Economic Education, 1995) (www.FEE.org. Compiled by Robert Gorgoglione) Used by permission.

6. List the three reasons the author mentions as reasons government should be limited. _____

7. What does the author say is the distinctive thing about the Constitution? _____

8. Which of the first ten amendments does the author consider the "crowning" one and why? _____

9. Some Americans would disagree with the author's last paragraph. Do you agree or disagree with his viewpoint? Explain your answer. _____

AMERICAN GOVERNMENT

Name _____

CHAPTER 4 • ACTIVITY 4

Patrick Henry, Anti-Federalist

On June 5 and 7, 1788, Patrick Henry, the firebrand of the War for Independence, famous for his "Give me liberty or give me death" speech, addressed the Virginia Ratifying Convention. This body had assembled to discuss whether Virginia should reject or ratify the Constitution. Henry opposed adopting the proposed Constitution. Read the following excerpts from his speeches, looking particularly for his reasons for holding that position. Then answer the questions that follow.

   Liberty, [is] the greatest of all earthly blessings—give us that precious jewel, and you may take every thing else! . . .

   But, Sir, suspicion is a virtue, as long as its object is the preservation of the public good. . . . Let your suspicion look to both sides. . . . Guard with jealous attention the public liberty. Suspect every one who approaches that jewel. . . . Consider what you are about to do before you part with this Government [of the Articles of Confederation]. Take longer time in reckoning things: Revolutions like this have happened in almost every country in Europe: Similar examples are to be found in ancient Greece and ancient Rome: Instances of the people losing their liberty by their own carelessness and the ambition of a few. . . . I acknowledge that licentiousness [lawlessness, disorder] is dangerous, and that it ought to be provided against: I acknowledge also the new form of Government [the Constitution] may effectually prevent it: Yet, there is another thing it will as effectually do: it will oppress and ruin the people. . . .

   But we are told that we need not fear, because those in power being our Representatives, will not abuse the powers we put in their hands: I am not well versed in history, but I will submit to your recollection, whether liberty has been destroyed most often by the licentiousness of the people, or by the tyranny of rulers? I imagine, Sir, you will find the balance on the side of tyranny. . . . And those nations who have gone in search of grandeur, power and splendor, have . . . been the victims of their own folly: . . . they lost their freedom. My great objection to this Government is, that it does not leave us the means of defending our rights; or, of waging war against tyrants. . . .

   What, Sir, is the genius of democracy? Let me read that clause of the Bill of Rights of Virginia, which relates to this: third clause, "That Government is or ought to be instituted for the common benefit, protection, and security of the people, nation, or community: Of all the various modes and forms of Government, that is best which is capable of producing the greatest degree of happiness and safety, and is most effectually secured against the danger of maladministration, and that whenever any Government shall be found inadequate, or contrary to these purposes, a majority of the community hath, an undubitable, unalienable and indefeasible right to reform, alter, or abolish it, in such manner as shall be judged most conducive to the public weal [well-being]." This, Sir, is the language of democracy; that a majority of the community have a right to alter their Government when found to be oppressive: . . .

1. What does Henry declare to be the greatest earthly blessing? Do you agree? Why? _____
   _____
   _____
   _____
   _____

2. What does he say is a virtue in relation to one's attitude toward government? _____
   _____

(continued on next page)

3. What does he believe has historically been the downfall of nations? _____

4. According to Henry, what do people have the right to do when government is inadequate or oppressive?
   _____

[T]here is one thing in it which I never would acquiesce in. I mean the changing it into a Consolidated Government; which is so abhorrent to my mind. . . . If we admit this Consolidated Government it will be because we like a great splendid one. Some way or other we must be a great and mighty empire; we must have an army, and a navy, and a number of things: When the American spirit was in its youth, the language of America was different: Liberty, Sir, was then the primary object. . . .

But now, Sir, the American spirit, assisted by the ropes and chains of consolidation, is about to convert this country to a powerful and mighty empire: If you make the citizens of this country agree to become the subjects of one great consolidated empire of America, your Government will not have sufficient energy to keep them together: Such a Government is incompatible with the genius of republicanism. . . .

Let us consider the latent consequences of an erroneous decision—and let not our minds be led away by unfair misrepresentations and uncandid suggestions. . . .

[T]his Constitution can counteract and suspend any of our laws, that contravene [conflict with] its oppressive operation; they have the power of direct taxation; which suspends our Bill of Rights; and it is expressly provided, that they can make all laws necessary for carrying their powers into execution; and it is declared paramount [supreme] to the laws and constitutions of the States. . . . So that the whole of our property may be taken by this American Government, by laying what taxes they please, giving themselves what salaries they please, and suspending our laws at their pleasure. . . .

It is on a supposition that our . . . [government leaders] shall be honest, that all the good qualities of this Government are founded: But its defective, and imperfect construction, puts it in their power to perpetrate the worst of mischiefs, should they be bad men. . . . If your American chief be a man of ambition, and abilities, how easy is it for him to render himself absolute: The army is in his hands, and, if he be a man of address, it will be attached to him; and it will be the subject of long meditation with him to seize the first auspicious moment to accomplish his design; and, Sir, will the American spirit solely relieve you when this happens?

Ralph Ketcham, ed. *The Anti-Federalist Papers and the Constitutional Convention Debates*, "Patrick Henry (June 5 and 7, 1788)." New York: Penguin Putnam Inc., 1986 (pp. 200–202, 204–5, 207–8, 210–11, 214).

5. Summarize Henry's arguments in the first two paragraphs on this page. _____
   _____
   _____
   _____

6. Summarize the last paragraph. _____
   _____
   _____
   _____

7. Do you agree or disagree with Henry's arguments in the final paragraph? Explain your answer.
   _____
   _____
   _____

AMERICAN GOVERNMENT

CHAPTER 4 • ACTIVITY 5

Name _____

Chapter Review

Answer the following questions.

1. What two significant events shook colonial America and encouraged independence? _____

2. What law, passed by Parliament in 1765, was the beginning of a series of taxes and trade restrictions on the colonies? _____

3. What is a boycott, and why did the colonists institute one? _____

4. Which assembly adopted the Declaration of Independence? _____

5. What were the four major truths Jefferson presented in the Declaration of Independence? _____

6. Which English Enlightenment philosopher most profoundly influenced America's Founding Fathers? _____

7. After declaring independence, what did the Second Continental Congress endeavor to establish? What was the result? _____

8. Why was it so difficult to obtain ratification for the Articles of Confederation? _____

9. What two events showed the states that their national union under the Articles of Confederation needed to be redefined, and how did these events illustrate this need? _____

(continued on next page)

10. Which assembly was convened on May 25, 1787? Who was chosen to lead the group? _____

11. What two procedural rules were adopted at the beginning of the Constitutional Convention? Why were these important? _____

12. Which three very difficult issues confronted the Constitutional Convention? _____

13. What did the Virginia Plan advocate, and which states did it favor? _____

14. What did the New Jersey Plan advocate, and which states did it favor? _____

15. Who proposed the Connecticut Compromise? _____

16. What was another name for the Connecticut Compromise? What did it propose? _____

17. What was the Three-Fifths Compromise? _____

18. Define the terms *Federalists* and *Anti-Federalists*. _____

19. Name three Federalist leaders and three Anti-Federalist leaders during the fight over ratification of the Constitution. _____

20. In which two states did the toughest ratification battles occur? _____

AMERICAN GOVERNMENT

Name _____

CHAPTER 5 • ACTIVITY 1

Why Was the Constitution Written?

Below the Preamble are excerpts from *A Familiar Exposition of the Constitution of the United States* by Joseph Story, who served as an associate justice on the US Supreme Court from 1812 to 1845. Story notes that the Constitution's Preamble states six purposes, or objects, for the writing of the Constitution.

After reading the Preamble, read Joseph Story's comments about those purposes. Then answer the accompanying questions.

Preamble

We the people of the United States, in order to form a more perfect union, establish justice, insure domestic tranquility, provide for the common defence, promote the general welfare, and secure the blessings of liberty to ourselves and our posterity, do ordain and establish this Constitution for the United States of America.

Joseph Story's Comments

[W]e are now prepared to enter upon an examination of the actual structure and organization of that Constitution, and the powers belonging to it. . . .

[The] Preamble is very important, not only as explanatory of the motives and objects [purposes] of framing the Constitution; but, as affording the best key to the true interpretation thereof. . . .

Every provision in the [Constitution] . . . may therefore fairly be presumed to have reference to one or more of these objects [purposes].

1. Summarize what Story is saying here. _____
   _____
   _____

The first object [purpose of the document] is, "to form a more perfect union." From what has been already stated, respecting the defects of the [government under the Articles of] Confederation, it is obvious, that a further continuance of the Union was impracticable, unless a new government was formed. . . .

The next object is, "to establish justice." This, indeed, is the first object of all good and rational forms of government. Without justice being fully, freely, and impartially administered, neither our persons, nor our rights, nor our property, can be protected. . . .

The next object is, "to insure domestic tranquility." From what has been already stated, it is apparent, how essential an efficient National Government is, to the security of the States against foreign influence, domestic dissensions, commercial rivalries, legislative retaliations, territorial disputes, and the perpetual irritations of a border warfare. . . .

2. List the first three objects, or purposes, that are given in the Preamble. Explain what they mean.
   _____
   _____
   _____
   _____

3. What does Story say about continuing the Union [the nation] as it existed under the Articles of Confederation? _____

(continued on next page)

The next object is "to provide for the common defence." One of the surest means of preserving peace is always to be prepared for war. . . .

The next object is "to promote the general welfare." If it should be asked, why this may not be effectually accomplished by the States, it may be answered; first, that they do not possess the means; and secondly, if they did, they do not possess the powers necessary to carry the appropriate measures into execution. . . .

After one or two vain attempts [by the States] to accomplish any great system of improvements, there would be a general abandonment of all efforts to produce a general system for the regulation of our commerce, or agriculture, or manufactures; and each State would be driven to consult its own peculiar convenience and policy only, in despair of any common concert. . . .

4. What two purposes of the Constitution are mentioned here? _____
   _____

5. Summarize this section. _____
   _____
   _____
   _____
   _____
   _____
   _____
   _____

The concluding object, stated in the Preamble, is "to secure the blessings of liberty to us [ourselves], and our posterity [descendants]." And surely nothing of mere earthly concern is more worthy of the profound reflection of wise and good men, than to erect structures of government, which shall permanently sustain the interests of civil, political, and religious liberty, on solid foundations. . . .

6. What is the concluding purpose of the Constitution that is stated in the Preamble? _____
   _____

The Constitution of the United States aims at the attainment of these ends, by the arrangements and distributions of its powers; by the introduction of checks and balances in all its departments . . . [and] by leaving with the States the ordinary powers of domestic legislation.

Joseph Story, *A Familiar Exposition of the Constitution of the United States* (New York: Harper, 1847), 36–38, 40, 42, 44–45.

7. In Chapter 5 of the textbook, six foundational principles of the Constitution are mentioned. Which three are noted in this last excerpt from Story? _____
   _____

AMERICAN GOVERNMENT

CHAPTER 5 • ACTIVITY 2

Strict or Broad Constructionist?

Read the quotations below. The first four are from US Supreme Court justices. The last is from Robert Bork, a judge on the US Court of Appeals. Identify whether the quotation indicates a strict or a broad constructionist view of the Constitution. Explain your answer.

"This Court inescapably has the duty, as the ultimate arbiter [mediator] of the meaning of our Constitution, to say whether, when individuals condemned to death stand before our bar, 'moral concepts' require us to hold that the law has progressed to the point where we should declare that the punishment of death, like punishments on the rack, the screw and the wheel [torture devices], is no longer morally tolerable in our society." —William J. Brennan Jr.

___

"Our Constitution was not written in the sands to be washed away by each wave of new judges blown in by each successive political wind." —Hugo L. Black

___

"Judges rule on the basis of law, not public opinion, and they should be totally indifferent to pressures of the times." —Warren E. Burger

___

"We deal with a right of privacy older than the Bill of Rights—older than our political parties, older than our school system." —William O. Douglas

___

"There is no other sense in which the Constitution can be what article VI proclaims it to be: 'Law. . . .' This means, of course, that a judge, no matter on what court he sits, may never create new constitutional rights or destroy old ones. Any time he does so, he violates not only the limits to his own authority but, and for that reason, also violates the rights of the legislature and the people. . . . [T]he philosophy of original understanding is thus a necessary inference from the structure of government apparent on the face of the Constitution." —Robert Bork

___

AMERICAN GOVERNMENT

CHAPTER 5 • ACTIVITY 3

Name _____

Popular Sovereignty

The following excerpt on popular sovereignty is from Alexis de Tocqueville's book *Democracy in America*. After reading it, complete the questions.

    I have already said that, from their origin, the sovereignty of the people was the fundamental principle of most of the British colonies in America. It was far, however, from then exercising as much influence on the government of society as it now does.

    It could not ostensibly [officially] disclose itself in the laws of colonies which were still forced to obey the mother country; it was therefore obliged to rule secretly in the provincial assemblies, and especially in the townships.

    American society at that time was not yet prepared to adopt it with all its consequences. Intelligence in New England and wealth in the country to the south of the Hudson [River] . . . long exercised a sort of aristocratic influence, which tended to keep the exercise of social power in the hands of a few. Not all the public functionaries [officials] were chosen by popular vote, nor were all the citizens voters. The electoral franchise [right to vote] was everywhere somewhat restricted and made dependent on a certain qualification [property ownership], which was very low in the North and more considerable in the South.

    The American Revolution broke out, and the doctrine of the sovereignty of the people came out of the townships and took possession of the [government]. Every class was enlisted in its cause; battles were fought and victories obtained for it; it became the law of laws. . . .

    In the present day [a half century after the American Revolution] the principle of the sovereignty of the people has acquired in the United States all the practical development that the imagination can conceive. . . . It appears in every possible form, according to the exigency [need] of the occasion. Sometimes the laws are made by the people in a body, as at Athens; and sometimes its representatives, chosen by universal suffrage, transact business in its name and under its immediate supervision. . . . The people reign in the American political world as the Deity does in the universe. They are the cause and the aim of all things; everything comes from them, and everything is absorbed in them.

1. Summarize Tocqueville's thoughts on America's popular sovereignty before, during, and after the American Revolution. _____

2. Evaluate popular sovereignty in light of the last two statements in the excerpt. _____

AMERICAN GOVERNMENT

Name _____

CHAPTER 5 • ACTIVITY 4

Differing Viewpoints Regarding Judicial Review

Read the introductory material below, entitled "Opposing Opinions." Then read the remarks from two Supreme Court justices and answer the questions.

Opposing Opinions

Justices on the US Supreme Court have varying viewpoints regarding how judges should make decisions. Two recent justices, Antonin Scalia (who served from 1986 until his death in 2016) and Stephen Breyer (a current justice who has been serving since 1994), wrote books that explained their judicial philosophy.

Scalia argued that the judge's task is to interpret the text of the Constitution or the law within its original context. The judge, he says, should not seek a desired outcome; he should just interpret the text. Scalia believed this approach to be essential to democracy. It ensures that the law is created by the people's representatives rather than created and recreated by judges.

Breyer's view is that, in addition to looking at the text of the Constitution or the law, a judge should consider the purpose for its writing. For example, since he believes that the goal of the Constitution is to promote democracy and to expand freedom, he states that a judge should factor into his decision whether his judgment strengthens those two items. Thus, the judge should not limit himself to the mere words of the Constitution or law.

One area in which the differences between these two justices is evident is in their conflicting view of laws regarding limiting the money that can be donated to political campaigns. Breyer has been willing to uphold laws that limit the money because such limitations promote democracy (by curbing the influence of the wealthy). On the other hand, Scalia opposed such laws because he believed they limited free speech and therefore violated the First Amendment.

1. Who was Antonin Scalia? _____

2. Who is Stephen Breyer? _____

3. Briefly explain how these two justices have differing views on the role of judges. _____

4. In your opinion, which justice had the correct approach to laws dealing with contributions to political campaigns? Explain your answer. _____

(continued on next page)

Justice Breyer Speaks

For one thing, emphasis matters when judges face difficult questions. . . . All judges use similar basic tools to help them accomplish the task. They read the text's language. . . . They take account of its history, including history that shows what the language likely meant to those who wrote it. They look to tradition indicating how the relevant language was, and is, used in the law. They examine precedents [previous legal decisions on the matter]. . . . They try to understand the phrase's purposes, . . . and they consider the likely consequences of the interpretive alternatives. . . . But the fact that most judges agree that these basic elements—language, history, tradition, precedent, purpose, and consequence—are useful does not mean they agree about just where and how to use them. Some judges emphasize the use of language, history, and tradition. Others emphasize purpose and consequence. These differences of emphasis matter. . . .

[My approach is to] see texts as driven by purposes. The judge should try to find and "honestly . . . say what was the underlying purpose expressed" in a statute. . . . The judge should recognize that the Constitution will apply to "new subject matter . . . with which the framers were not familiar." Thus, the judge . . . should "reconstruct the past solution imaginatively in its setting and project the purposes" [upon the present situation].

Stephen Breyer, *Active Liberty: Interpreting Our Democratic Constitution* (New York: Knopf, 2005), 7–8, 17–18.

5. What six basic elements does Breyer say all judges consider when attempting to interpret a law or the Constitution? He summarizes each with one word. _____

6. Explain the approach Breyer advocates. _____

Justice Scalia Speaks

[I]t is simply incompatible with democratic government, or indeed, even with fair government, to have the meaning of a law determined by what the lawgiver meant, rather than by what the lawgiver promulgated [declared]. . . . It is the law that governs, not the intent of the lawgiver. . . . [We are] a government of laws, not of men. Men may intend what they will; but it is only the laws that they enact which bind us. . . .

The philosophy of interpretation I have described above is known as textualism. . . .

Words do have a limited range of meaning, and no interpretation that goes beyond that range is permissible. . . .

I do not suggest, mind you, that originalists [those who support textualism] always agree upon their answer. There is plenty of room for disagreement as to what original meaning was, and even more as to how that original meaning applies to the situation before the court. But the originalist at least knows what he is looking for: the original meaning of the text. . . .

[T]he difficulties and uncertainties of determining original meaning and applying it to modern circumstances are negligible compared with the difficulties and uncertainties of the philosophy which says that the Constitution changes. . . .

Antonin Scalia, *A Matter of Interpretation: Federal Courts and the Law* (Princeton, NJ: Princeton University Press, 1997), 17, 23–24, 45.

7. What does Scalia say is incompatible with democratic government? Explain his remarks. _____

8. Explain the two views Scalia is contrasting in the last two paragraphs of the excerpt. _____

AMERICAN GOVERNMENT

Name _____

CHAPTER 5 • ACTIVITY 5

Chapter Review

Use your textbook or the text of the Constitution itself to identify the following.

1. Those who believe that closely following the text of the Constitution is important and that any interpretation should be kept to a minimum _____

2. Those who take a more flexible approach to interpreting the Constitution _____

3. Added by the Constitution's framers so that future Congresses would have authority to complete future tasks _____

4. The formal introduction of a constitutional amendment _____

5. The formal approval process for an amendment _____

6. Number of amendments that have been adopted _____

7. First ten amendments to the Constitution _____

8. Six basic principles found in the Constitution _____

9. Formally charging the president with misconduct _____

10. Political stalemate or deadlock _____

11. The power of the courts to consider the constitutionality of laws passed by the legislative branch _____

12. The division of power between national and state levels of government _____

13. Belief that the people are the ultimate source of their government's authority _____

14. Introduces the Constitution by explaining its nature and purpose _____

15. The six purposes of the Constitution according to the Preamble _____

16. Branch of government whose primary function is to make laws _____

(continued on next page)

17. A two-house legislative system _____

18. Leader elected by the Senate who serves as the leader of that group when the vice president is absent _____

19. The minimum number of members needed to transact business _____

20. The journal of the daily proceedings in each house of Congress _____

21. The right to send official mail free of charge _____

22. Occurs when the president does not sign a bill and Congress adjourns within ten days _____

23. The process whereby a foreign-born person gains US citizenship _____

24. Forces authorities to charge an arrested person quickly or to release him _____

25. Money allocated by Congress for a certain purpose _____

26. Branch of government whose primary function is to enforce the nation's laws _____

27. The group of elected representatives from each state that elects the president _____

28. Temporary postponement of punishment _____

29. Complete forgiveness for a crime and its consequent punishment _____

30. The branch whose function is to interpret the law _____

31. A court's power to hear a case before that case is considered by any other court _____

32. A court's power to decide a case that was originally in a lower court _____

33. Crime that requires a confession or two eyewitnesses for conviction _____

34. The legal process of returning a criminal to the state in which he has been charged with a crime _____

35. Constitutional provision that upholds the US Constitution, federal laws, and treaties as the highest law of the nation _____

36. Defaming a person verbally _____

37. Defaming a person in writing _____

38. Money paid to guarantee a court appearance, allowing the accused to be free while awaiting trial _____

39. Two words meaning the right to vote _____

40. Tax required before a person could vote _____

AMERICAN GOVERNMENT

CHAPTER 6 • ACTIVITY 1

Name _____

Federalism's Development

Use your textbook and outside sources to complete the chart by writing the description of each event or piece of legislation as well as the impact on the development of US federalism.

Event/Legislation	Description	Impact on development of US federalism
United States Constitution (1787)		
McCulloch v. Maryland (1819)		
Civil War (1861–65)		
Morrill Act (1862)		

(continued on next page)

Event/Legislation	Description	Impact on development of US federalism
Interstate Commerce Act (1887) and Sherman Antitrust Act (1890)		
Sixteenth Amendment (1913)		
New Deal (1930s)		
Great Society (1960s)		
New Federalism (1980s)		

AMERICAN GOVERNMENT

Name _____

CHAPTER 6 • ACTIVITY 2

Revenue Sharing

Read the following two statements about revenue sharing. Then answer the questions that follow.

Under Nixon

Following is the statement by Nixon during the ceremony in which he signed the revenue sharing bill in Independence Hall in Philadelphia, October 20, 1972.

In my State of the Union Address nearly two years ago, I outlined a program which I described as "a new American revolution—a peaceful revolution in which power [is] turned back to the people. . . ."

The signing today of the State and Local Fiscal Assistance Act of 1972—the legislation known as general revenue sharing—means that this new American revolution is truly under way. . . .

After many years in which power has been flowing away from those levels of government which are closest to the people, power will now begin to flow back to the people again—a development which can have an enormous impact on their daily existence. . . .

But the most important point is this: In each case it will be local officials responding to local conditions and local constituencies who will decide what should happen, and not some distant bureaucrat in Washington, DC.

The American people are fed up with government that doesn't deliver. Revenue sharing can help State and local government deliver again, closing the gap between promise and performance.

Revenue sharing will give these hard-pressed governments the dollars they need so badly. But just as importantly, it will give them the freedom they need to use those dollars as effectively as possible.

Under this program, instead of spending so much time trying to please distant bureaucrats in Washington—so the money will keep coming in—State and local officials can concentrate on pleasing the people—so the money can do more good. . . .

. . . When we say no strings, we mean no strings. This program will mean both a new source of revenue for State and local governments and a new sense of responsibility. . . .

Richard Nixon: "Statement About the General Revenue Sharing Bill", October 20, 1972. Online by Gerhard Peters and John T. Woolley, The American Presidency Project. http://www.presidency.ucsb.edu/node/255247

Under Reagan

Following is a report by The Heritage Foundation explaining and defending Reagan's rationale for making drastic cuts in, and eventually ending, the revenue sharing program.

. . . Declared Ronald Reagan to the nation's governors at their annual Washington meeting last month: "There is simply no justification for the federal government, which is running a [yearly budget] deficit, to be borrowing money to be spent by state and local governments." As such, Reagan's proposed FY 1986 budget slashes Revenue Sharing by 80 percent and eventually will eliminate it altogether.

The original rationale for the program has evaporated completely because of changed financial circumstances. . . .

Revenue Sharing has represented unwise federalism policy from its inception. At last, time has run out for the program, and it should be eliminated. . . .

The size of the grant is determined by a statutorily set formula which divides the total Revenue Sharing funds appropriated by Congress among the eligible recipients. Basically, the formula provides funds to recipient governments according to their population. It also awards

(continued on next page)

extra funds if a locality's per capita income is low and if its tax revenues are high relative to local income (a relation known as tax effort). . . .

Changing circumstances have nullified the original Revenue Sharing rationale. It is now the federal government which is in deep financial trouble, while state and local governments generally are far more robust. . . .

For the debt-ridden federal government to be "sharing revenue" with states in financial surplus is like bankrupt Argentina providing assistance to oil-rich Saudi Arabia. State and local governments easily could absorb the loss of Federal Revenue Sharing grants, since all but Delaware have their own revenue sharing programs for local governments and thus could assist these governments if the loss of federal funds posed a particular problem. . . .

State and local government services, such as local roadways and fire protection, should be financed primarily by funds raised at the state and local levels—just as national programs, such as defense, should be financed at the federal level. If the benefits of a particular local service or project are worth the cost, then the local citizens who benefit will be willing to tax themselves to pay for it. If they are not willing to do so, this is strong indication that the costs are not worth the benefits, and the service or project should not be undertaken. . . .

Federal Revenue Sharing fails to conform to the principles of federalism. It does not seek to promote a clear national purpose with national funds. The activities supported with federal money are state and local concerns, and so should be funded by those levels of government. Revenue Sharing adopts the rhetoric and façade of federalism without really attempting to accomplish the difficult tasks necessary to restore the historic balance among different levels of government. The program is itself part of the federalism problem.

Peter J. Ferrara. "For Revenue Sharing, Time Has Run Out." *The Heritage Foundation Backgrounder,* March 13, 1985.

1. Which of the two presidents' plans do you think was right? Defend your answer. _____

2. Summarize the direct quote from President Reagan. _____

3. What seemed to be Nixon's primary "selling point" for the states in his original proposal? _____

4. What did the second excerpt put forth as a good example of the legitimate expenditure of national revenues? _____

5. Which of these plans—Nixon's or Reagan's—represents true federalism as the framers of the Constitution intended it? Defend your answer. _____

AMERICAN GOVERNMENT

CHAPTER 6 • ACTIVITY 3

A Brief History of American Federalism

Ellis Katz was a professor at Temple University in Philadelphia. Below are excerpts from one of his articles. Read the information and answer the questions that follow.

When the 13 North American colonies declared their independence from Great Britain on July 4, 1776, they recognized the need to coordinate their efforts in the war and to cooperate with each other generally. To these ends, they adopted the Articles of Confederation. . . . The Articles were barely sufficient to hold the states together through the war against England and, at the successful conclusion of that war, fell apart completely as the states pursued their own interests rather than the national interest of the new United States.

To remedy the defects of the Articles . . . [American] leaders called upon the states to send delegates to a constitutional convention to meet in the city of Philadelphia in May 1787. . . .

The framers of the Constitution rejected both confederal and unitary models of government. Instead, they based the new American government on an entirely new theory: federalism. In a confederation . . . sovereignty remains with the states. . . . In a unitary system, on the other hand, the national government is sovereign and the states, if they exist at all, are mere administrative arms of the central government. In the American federal system, the people retain their basic sovereignty and they delegate some powers to the national government and reserve other powers to the states. . . .

1. List and describe the two models of government that the framers of the Constitution rejected.

   _____
   _____
   _____

2. List and describe the model the framers devised. _____

   _____
   _____

The first 75 years of American development (1790–1865) were marked by constitutional and political conflicts about the nature of American federalism. Almost immediately George Washington, Alexander Hamilton, John Marshall and their Federalist colleagues argued for an expansive interpretation of federal authority, while Thomas Jefferson, James Madison, Spencer Roane and their partisan allies maintained that the American union was little more than a confederation in which power and sovereignty remained with the states. . . .

The American Civil War (1860–65) did much to resolve these federalism questions. The northern victory and the subsequent adoption of the 13th, 14th and 15th amendments to the Constitution . . . established the supremacy of the national Constitution and laws over the states . . . .

3. Explain the conflicts that occurred during the first 75 years after the Constitution was adopted.

   _____

4. Describe the effect the Civil War and its aftermath had on federalism. _____

   _____
   _____
   _____

(continued on next page)

Two [twentieth century] developments, however, led to the expansion of federal authority, and, according to some critics, brought about an imbalance in American federalism.... Under the New Deal programs of President Franklin D. Roosevelt [which attempted to deal with the economic crisis of the Great Depression], the functions of the federal government expanded enormously.... Many of these programs, while funded by the federal government, were administered by the states, giving rise to the federal grant-in-aid system [whereby the federal government gives federal tax money to the states to spend in their state budgets]....

Until the New Deal, the prevailing concept of federalism was "dual federalism," a system in which the national government and the states have totally separate sets of responsibilities. Thus foreign affairs and national defense were the business of the federal government alone, while education and family law were matters for the states exclusively. The New Deal broke this artificial distinction....

Under President Lyndon B. Johnson's [programs known as the] Great Society ... federal funds were now often given directly to units of local government—counties, cities, small towns, and school and other special districts.... The Great Society reached almost every policy area—education, police and fire protection, historic preservation, public libraries, infant health care, urban renewal, public parks and recreation, sewage and water systems and public transit....

5. List and describe the two twentieth-century developments that led to an expansion of federal authority.

6. The author notes that some critics say that the two developments mentioned brought an imbalance to American federalism. Why do you agree or disagree?

President Richard M. Nixon tried to fix all of this by the consolidation of small categorical grant programs into larger bloc grant programs in which the states would have more discretion. By and large, however, his efforts failed.... The presidency of Ronald Reagan seemed to promise a solution. While Reagan supported many of Nixon's proposed solutions, his real impact was on federal spending, which has caused Americans to re-think not only federalism, but the role of government itself.

Wanting a smaller role for government, especially for the federal government, Reagan successfully fought for increased defense spending, tax cuts and increased (or at least maintained) levels of Social Security payments. The result was that there was less and less money available for federal domestic grant-in-aid programs....

American federalism was never merely a set of static [immoveable] institutional arrangements, frozen in time by the US Constitution. Rather, American federalism is a dynamic, multi-dimensional process that has economic, administrative, and political aspects as well as constitutional ones....

Ellis Katz, "American Federalism, Past, Present, and Future," *Issues of Democracy*, USIA Electronic Journals, Vol. 2, No. 2, April 1997.

7. Discuss President Reagan's beliefs about the role of government.

8. What were the results of President Reagan's efforts?

9. Summarize the author's concluding paragraph.

AMERICAN GOVERNMENT

Name _____

CHAPTER 6 • ACTIVITY 4

Chapter Review

Answer the following questions.

1. What is federalism? _____
_____
_____

2. What defines the limits of the authority of the national government? _____
_____

3. Define enumerated or expressed powers. _____
_____

4. What are not clearly stated in the Constitution's text but are derived from enumerated powers?
_____

5. What is the elastic clause? _____
_____
_____

6. What refers to powers the Constitution withholds from the national government but not from state governments? Where in the Constitution is this directive given? _____
_____

7. According to the supremacy clause, what three items are the supreme law of the land? _____
_____

8. Define dual federalism. _____
_____

9. Which amendment established a federal income tax? _____

10. What were the results of the Income Tax Amendment? _____
_____
_____

11. What was the term for FDR's programs that were implemented to address the problems of the Great Depression? _____

(continued on next page)

12. What was the term for President Lyndon Johnson's programs that were intended to address problems within the country? _____

13. What is a key force in implementing national policies on the local level? _____

14. Identify the term for federal programs that grant money to state and local governments for specific purposes. _____

15. What are the two types of categorical grants? _____

16. Which type of grant simplifies state or local administration of federal funds by providing more flexible stipulations? _____

17. What is the name for the means of distributing federal grants that began in 1972 and was dismantled in 1986? _____

18. List four requirements that are placed on the national government with regard to the states.

19. By withholding or reducing federal aid, the national government has pressured states to adopt certain laws and procedures. One example was the implementation of a maximum speed limit of 55 miles per hour (1974–1987). Name another issue in which the national government has exerted similar influence.

20. How does federalism protect against tyranny? _____

AMERICAN GOVERNMENT

Name _____

CHAPTER 7 • ACTIVITY 1

When There Is No Government

Read the following summary of what people did in the past when they had no government or when their government was too far removed to provide for the needs of the people locally. Then follow the instructions given at the end of the list of examples.

Many examples exist in history of situations in which the people of an area either did not have a government or had a government that was so far from their local area that it was powerless (or unwilling) to govern effectively. In such cases, the people, recognizing the absolute need for some form of government, formed de facto or quasi-governments (governments that existed though they were not the official government) to meet their need for law and order. Some of the most famous examples include the following.

The Pilgrims, upon arrival in the New World, agreed to the Mayflower Compact. It was written because the English government was a vast distance from their little colony and because they were settling in an area far north of Virginia (the area in which they had permission to live).

The people of what is now upper East Tennessee founded the Watauga Association. Later, settlers in the same area similarly founded the short-lived State of Franklin.

Other examples include the Green Mountain Colony in Vermont, the early settlers of Kentucky, the early Americans who settled in Texas, and the State of Deseret in what is today Utah.

Choose one of the preceding instances and research it more fully. Use the questions below to guide your research.

1. Which historical example of de facto or quasi-government will you research? _____

2. Describe the historical context that made the quasi-government necessary. _____
   _____
   _____
   _____
   _____
   _____
   _____
   _____

3. Describe the organization of the government formed and explain how it worked. _____
   _____
   _____
   _____
   _____
   _____
   _____

(continued on next page)

4. How long did the government last? Did it meet the original needs? Why? _____
   _____
   _____
   _____
   _____
   _____
   _____

5. What role (if any) did this quasi-government have in the formation of the permanent local or state government? _____
   _____
   _____
   _____
   _____
   _____
   _____

6. What conclusions can be drawn or lessons learned from this historical event? _____
   _____
   _____
   _____

7. Share your information in the form of a written report or slide presentation.

AMERICAN GOVERNMENT

Name _____

CHAPTER 7 • ACTIVITY 2

Researching Your State and Local Governments

Locate a copy of your state's constitution. Study it to find the answers to the following questions. Then use outside materials to research your county government and your municipal government to answer questions related to those and other local governments.

General

1. What is the name of your state? _____

2. When was your state's constitution adopted? _____

3. Does your state constitution have a preamble or a bill of rights—or both? List the stated rights.

   _____
   _____
   _____
   _____
   _____
   _____
   _____
   _____
   _____
   _____

4. List your state constitution's articles by number and title. List any amendments.

   _____
   _____
   _____
   _____
   _____
   _____
   _____
   _____
   _____
   _____

(continued on next page)

Legislative Branch

1. What are the names of your state's legislature, upper chamber, and lower chamber?

    Legislature _____

    Upper chamber _____

    Lower chamber _____

2. How many members are in your state's upper chamber? in the lower chamber? _____

3. Is the office of state legislator a full-time or a part-time job in your state? _____

4. In what lower chamber district do you live? Who is your state representative? _____
   _____

5. In what upper chamber district do you live? Who is your state senator? _____
   _____

Executive Branch

1. What is the name of your state's governor? Of which political party is he or she a member?
   _____

2. What is the name of your state's lieutenant governor? _____

3. What are the responsibilities of your state's lieutenant governor? _____
   _____
   _____

4. In your state, is the governorship a strong or a weak position? On what basis do you conclude that?
   _____
   _____
   _____

Judicial Branch

1. What is the name given to your state's highest court? _____

2. Where does that court conduct its sessions? _____

3. How many justices serve on that court? What are their names? _____
   _____
   _____

(continued on next page)

4. How are the justices selected? _____

5. Which justice is the Chief Justice? _____

6. What other courts are included in your state's judicial system? _____
_____

State Finances

1. What are the major sources of your state's revenue? What percentage of the total revenue is from each source? _____
_____
_____
_____

2. How are state expenditures divided? (Give the percentage of each major category.)
_____
_____
_____
_____

County Government

1. What is the name of the county/parish/borough where you live? _____

2. Describe the organization of your county government (executive, commission, etc.). _____
_____
_____
_____
_____

3. What is the name of your county executive? your commissioner/supervisor? _____
_____

4. What are the major county offices? (For each, indicate whether it is an elected or an appointed position.)
_____
_____
_____
_____
_____

(continued on next page)

Municipal Government

1. What is the name of the municipality where you live (or the nearest municipality)?

2. What type of government structure does it have (mayor-council, council-manager, other)?

3. What is the name of the mayor or manager?

4. What is the name of your councilman?

Political Organization

1. What is the name/number of the voting precinct or ward where you live?

2. What prominent political parties have organizations in your state and county?

3. Choose one of the political parties and list the name of that party's county chairman.

4. In your state, do political parties choose their candidates by a primary? If so, is the primary open, closed, or semi-closed?

5. Does your state permit recall? referendum? initiative?

AMERICAN GOVERNMENT

CHAPTER 7 • ACTIVITY 3

Eminent Domain

The excerpts below describe *Kelo v. City of New London*, a case involving eminent domain that was decided by the US Supreme Court in 2005. Complete the questions that follow.

The case originated with a development project in the Fort Trumbull area of New London, a small city in Connecticut. The neighborhood had fallen on difficult economic times in the 1990s after the closure of a naval research facility. City officials and others hoped to revitalize it. The administration of Republican Governor John Rowland hoped to expand his political base by promoting development in New London; but to avoid having to work directly through the heavily Democratic city government, they helped resuscitate the long-moribund New London Development Corporation [NLDC], a private nonprofit organization established to aid the city with development planning.

The NLDC produced a development plan that would revitalize Fort Trumbull by building housing, office space, and other facilities that would support a new headquarters that Pfizer, Inc.—a major pharmaceutical firm—had agreed to build nearby. The development plan produced by the NLDC was in large part based on Pfizer's requirements, which NLDC leaders (some of whom had close ties to Pfizer) were eager to meet. Pfizer would not be the new owner of the redeveloped land, but did expect to benefit from it. I believe that NLDC leaders genuinely thought the plan would serve the public interest, as did city and state officials who supported it. But it is also true, as one of those who worked on the plan put it, that Pfizer was the "10,000 pound gorilla" behind the project.

In order to implement the plan, the NLDC sought to acquire land belonging to some ninety different Fort Trumbull property owners. In 2000, the New London city council authorized the NLDC to use eminent domain to condemn the land of those who refused to sell. Some defenders of the takings emphasize that all but seven of the owners sold "voluntarily." But as New London's counsel Wesley Horton noted in oral argument before the Supreme Court, many did so because there was "always in the background the possibility of being able to condemn . . . that obviously facilitates a lot of voluntary sales." Moreover, owners who were reluctant to sell were subjected to considerable harassment, such as late night phone calls, dumping of waste on their property, and locking out tenants during cold winter weather.

Seven individuals and families, who between them owned fifteen residential properties, refused to sell despite the pressure. One was Susette Kelo, who wanted to hold on to her "little pink house" near the waterfront. Some of the other families involved had deep roots in the community and did not want to be forced out. Wilhelmina Dery, who was in her eighties, had lived in the same house her whole life, and wished to continue living there during the time left to her. The Cristofaro family were also strongly attached to their property, which they had purchased in the 1970s after their previous home had been condemned as part of an urban renewal project.

The resisting property owners tried to use the political process to prevent the takings. They managed to attract the support of a wide range of people in the community, including many on the political left who believed that it was wrong to forcibly expel people from their homes in order to promote commercial development. But the Coalition to Save Fort Trumbull organized by the resisters and their allies had little, if any, hope of prevailing against the vastly more powerful forces arrayed against them.

The owners also tried to hire lawyers to fight the taking in court. But the lawyers they approached told them that there was little chance of success, and that—in any event—they could not afford the necessary prolonged legal battle.

1. How many property owners were affected by the NLDC plan? How many refused to sell their property?

   _____

2. Describe the viewpoints of Susette Kelo, Wilhelmina Dery, and the Cristofaro family. _____

   _____

   _____

(continued on next page)

The owners would almost certainly have had to capitulate, if not for the intervention of the Institute for Justice [IJ], a libertarian public interest firm contacted by one of the members of the Coalition. IJ had long been interested in promoting stronger judicial enforcement of "public use" limitations on takings.

As IJ lawyer Scott Bullock put it, the Fort Trumbull situation was an "ideal public interest case" for the Institute. Legally, the case was a good one because the city did not claim that the property in question was "blighted" or otherwise causing harm, thereby making it harder to prove that condemnation would genuinely benefit the public. The case also featured sympathetic plaintiffs who were determined to fight for their rights. That made it likely that it would play well in the court of public opinion, and that it would not be settled before it could lead to a precedent-setting decision. IJ hoped to achieve a ruling holding that takings that transfer property from one private individual to another for "economic development" do not serve a genuine "public use" and are therefore unconstitutional.

Thanks to IJ's pro bono legal representation, the case went to trial. In 2002, a Connecticut trial court invalidated the condemnation of 11 of the 15 properties because the city and the NLDC did not have a clear enough plan of what they intended to do with the land. Both sides appealed to the Connecticut Supreme Court, which upheld all fifteen takings in a close 4-3 decision. The majority ruled that almost any public benefit counts as a "public use" under the state and federal constitutions, and that courts must generally defer to government planners. . . .

At this point, most legal commentators (myself included) believed that the case was almost certainly over. Few thought that the federal Supreme Court was going to take a public use case. Supreme Court precedent dating back to 1954 held that virtually any possible public benefit counts as a public use, and the Court had unanimously reaffirmed that view in 1984. Most experts thought that the debate over the meaning of "public use" had been definitively settled.

But Scott Bullock and Dana Berliner—the IJ lawyers who represented the property owners—thought the conventional wisdom was wrong. And they were vindicated when the Supreme Court unexpectedly agreed to take the case. At that point, much new national media attention was focused on the New London condemnations.

Property law experts were well aware that longstanding Supreme Court precedent permitted the government to take property for almost any reason. But very few members of the general public knew that. Many ordinary Americans were shocked to learn a city could condemn homes and small businesses in order to promote private development—a reality they were unaware of until the publicity surrounding *Kelo* drove it home to them.

The Supreme Court upheld the takings in a 5-4 ruling. But the resulting controversy created a major political backlash and shattered the seeming consensus in favor of a broad approach to public use. . . .

The NLDC's flawed development plan fell through, as did a number of later efforts. Richard Palmer, one of the state supreme court justices who voted with the majority, later apologized to Susette Kelo, telling her he "would have voted differently" had he known what would happen.

Today, the condemned land still lies empty, though city officials now plan to build a memorial park honoring the victims of eminent domain, on the former site of Susette Kelo's house.

Ilya Somin, "The Story Behind *Kelo v. City of New London*—How an Obscure Takings Case Got to the Supreme Court and Shocked the Nation," *Volokh Conspiracy* (blog), *Washington Post*, May 29, 2015. Used by permission.

3. What did the US Supreme Court rule in this case? What did the resulting controversy create?

_____

_____

_____

4. What do you think are some possible long-term consequences if government has unlimited use of eminent domain? _____

_____

_____

AMERICAN GOVERNMENT

Name _____

CHAPTER 7 • ACTIVITY 4

Chapter Review

Write the appropriate terms in the spaces provided.

1. What is the name of a legislative body that has only one house? _____

2. What is the best example of direct democracy in the United States? (These are most common in New England.) _____

3. What term refers to the lowest level of a group or activity? _____

4. There are basically two types of elections. One is a primary election. What is the other?
   _____

5. In some states, if no candidate receives a majority of the votes in a primary election, what must occur between the two candidates that receive the most votes? _____

6. A few states use a primary system where all candidates, regardless of party affiliation, are listed on the ballot. What is this method called? _____

(continued on next page)

Match the following terms with their correct definitions or descriptions.

A. bicameral
B. closed primary
C. commission government
D. council-manager system
E. county
F. county executive
G. extradition
H. full faith and credit
I. governor
J. initiative
K. lieutenant governor
L. mayor-council system
M. municipalities
N. open primary
O. political machine
P. political party
Q. precinct
R. primary election
S. recall
T. reciprocity
U. special district
V. supreme court
W. Tenth Amendment
X. unified government
Y. winner-take-all primary

_____ 7. gives states the powers not delegated to the national government or prohibited to the states

_____ 8. having two chambers in the legislature

_____ 9. chief executive officer of a state

_____ 10. a state's secondary executive officer

_____ 11. the highest level of a state's judiciary system

_____ 12. subdivision of a state; in some states called a parish or a borough

_____ 13. sometimes called the "mayor" of a county

_____ 14. form of government whereby a county and a large city within that county share the same government to avoid duplication of services

_____ 15. urban, local systems of government including cities, villages, and towns

_____ 16. municipal governing system that has an executive authority who shares power with the individually elected members of a legislative authority

_____ 17. form of city government by which a legislative body passes laws that are enforced by a hired professional administrator

_____ 18. less common form of municipal government in which elected individuals oversee various aspects of the government

_____ 19. an independent government entity that provides specific functions or services within specified boundaries

_____ 20. a group that advances common goals and tries to win elections to implement those goals

_____ 21. the lowest level of political party organization

_____ 22. organization with an authoritarian leader or an elite group that demanded political loyalty

_____ 23. preliminary step whereby a party determines who its candidates will be in the general election

_____ 24. a party election in which voters do not have to declare their party membership but can vote in any primary race for any one party

_____ 25. a method of choosing candidates in which only members of the party can participate

_____ 26. process by which voters can remove an elected official from office

_____ 27. method for voters to propose changes to state constitution or laws

_____ 28. constitutional provision that requires states to respect each other's public acts, records, and judicial proceedings

_____ 29. legal process of returning an alleged criminal from one state to the state where he is charged

_____ 30. a means of cooperation between states whereby one state recognizes certain privileges stipulated by another state or states

AMERICAN GOVERNMENT

CHAPTER 8 • ACTIVITY 1

Name _____

Congress and Its Leaders

Part One: Which Person?

Identify the person who presently holds the following positions. Also, list the political party and the state of each person. This activity will require the use of outside resources.

Leaders in the House of Representatives

1. Majority Leader

    Name _____ Party _____ State _____

2. Majority Whip

    Name _____ Party _____ State _____

3. Minority Leader

    Name _____ Party _____ State _____

4. Minority Whip

    Name _____ Party _____ State _____

5. Speaker of the House

    Name _____ Party _____ State _____

Leaders in the Senate

6. Majority Leader

    Name _____ Party _____ State _____

7. Majority Whip

    Name _____ Party _____ State _____

8. Minority Leader

    Name _____ Party _____ State _____

9. Minority Whip

    Name _____ Party _____ State _____

10. President Pro Tempore

    Name _____ Party _____ State _____

(continued on next page)

11. Vice President (the President of the Senate)

    Name _____ Party _____ State _____

Part Two: Which Congress?

12. The 1st Congress held its first meeting in 1789; the 50th Congress held its first meeting in 1887; and the 75th Congress met for the first time in 1937. What is the number of the current Congress? _____

13. The current Congress began meeting in January of what year? _____

14. The next Congress will begin meeting in January of what year? _____

15. What will be the number of the next Congress? _____

Part Three: Which Requirements?

16. What are the three requirements for a person to serve in the House of Representatives? _____

17. What are the three requirements for a person to serve in the Senate? _____

Part Four: Women in Congress?

There is a feature box on page 174 of the textbook entitled "Women in Congress." Because of resignations, elections, and deaths, the number of women in Congress varies from year to year. Update the feature box on page 174 by researching the following questions.

18. How many women are presently in the House of Representatives? How many are from each political party?

19. How many women are presently in the Senate? How many are from each political party?

AMERICAN GOVERNMENT

CHAPTER 8 • ACTIVITY 2

Your Representative's and Senators' Committee Assignments

Use resources outside your textbook to identify your state's two US senators and the US representative from the congressional district in which you live. List the committees and subcommittees on which each of these officials serves. Identify each committee as a standing or joint committee, and identify any committees or subcommittees each might chair with a (C).

Senator	Senator	Representative
Committees	**Committees**	**Committees**
Subcommittees	**Subcommittees**	**Subcommittees**

AMERICAN GOVERNMENT

Name _____

CHAPTER 8 • ACTIVITY 3

A Bill Becomes Law

Describe each step of a bill's journey from introduction to law.

Step One: Introducing a Bill

_____
_____
_____
_____

Step Two: Committee Deliberation

_____
_____
_____
_____

Step Three: Full House Vote

_____
_____
_____
_____

Step Four: Conference Committee

_____
_____
_____
_____

Step Five: Presidential Signature

_____
_____
_____
_____

AMERICAN GOVERNMENT

CHAPTER 8 • ACTIVITY 4

Chapter Review

Answer the following questions.

1. What was created because of the Great Compromise at the Constitutional Convention? _____

2. What is an official count of a country's population called? _____

3. Define *reapportionment*. _____

4. Define *gerrymandering* and explain how it got its name. _____

5. What is the term for a geographical area in a state represented by a House member? _____

6. Define *single-member district*. _____

7. Which amendment changed the method of the election of senators? Explain the change. _____

8. What is a coalition? _____

9. Define *caucus*. What term do Republicans use instead of *caucus*? _____

10. What is the name of the position in the House and Senate for the leader of the party with the most members? _____

11. What is the name of the position in the House and the Senate for the leader of the party with the second most members? _____

12. Who are the assistant majority/minority congressional leaders, and what are their responsibilities? _____

(continued on next page)

13. Which position in the Senate is mainly honorary and is given to the most senior member of the Senate's majority party? _____

14. Which position in the House of Representatives is the only House position named in the Constitution? _____

15. Define *term limits*. _____

16. What is the franking privilege, and who uses it? _____

17. What do critics call unnecessary trips taken by members of Congress? _____

18. List the four different types of committees in Congress. _____

19. Which type of congressional committee is permanent and is more powerful than other types of committees? _____

20. Which type of congressional committee is permanent, is composed of House and Senate members, and serves as an advisory board to other congressional committees? _____

21. Which type of congressional committee is temporary and is drawn from both chambers to devise a compromise agreement on a bill? _____

22. Within congressional committees, who has the greatest power? _____

23. What is a filibuster, and which chamber of Congress uses it? _____

24. What is the motion to limit debate called? _____

25. Define *pocket veto*. _____

AMERICAN GOVERNMENT

Name _____

CHAPTER 9 • ACTIVITY 1

War Powers Resolution

Read the following sections from the War Powers Act that was passed by Congress in 1973. Then answer the questions that follow.

Resolved by the Senate and the House of Representatives of the United States of America in Congress assembled,

Purpose and Policy

Sec. 2 (a) It is the purpose of this joint resolution [act] to fulfill the intent of the framers of the Constitution of the United States and insure that the collective judgement of both the Congress and the President will apply to the introduction of United States Armed Forces into hostilities, or into situations where imminent involvement in hostilities is clearly indicated by the circumstances, and to the continued use of such forces in hostilities or in such situations.

(b) Under Article I, Section 8, of the Constitution, it is specifically provided that the Congress shall have the power to make all laws necessary and proper for carrying into execution, not only its own powers but also all other powers vested by the Constitution in the Government of the United States, or in any department or officer thereof.

(c) The constitutional powers of the President as Commander-in-Chief to introduce United States Armed Forces into hostilities, or into situations where imminent hostilities is clearly indicated by the circumstances, are exercised only pursuant to (1) a declaration of war, (2) specific statutory authorization [specific authorization by Congress], or (3) a national emergency created by attack upon the United States, its territories or possessions, or its armed forces.

Consultation

Sec. 3 The President in every possible instance shall consult with Congress before introducing United States Armed Forces into hostilities or into situation where imminent involvement in hostilities is clearly indicated by the circumstances, and after every such introduction shall consult regularly with the Congress until United States Armed Forces are no longer engaged in hostilities or have been removed from such situations.

1. According to the resolution, what is the purpose of the War Powers Resolution? _____
   _____

2. What is the resolution supposed to insure? _____
   _____

3. Where in the Constitution is power given to Congress to make and carry out the necessary laws pertaining to the US government or any department or officer of the government? _____

4. Describe the instances in which the president may send United States Armed Forces into hostilities or situations where hostilities might occur. _____
   _____
   _____

5. What must the president do, in every possible instance, before committing US forces into hostilities?
   _____

(continued on next page)

Reporting

Sec. 4 (a) In the absence of a declaration of war, in any case in which United States Armed Forces are introduced . . . the president shall submit within 48 hours to the Speaker of the House of Representatives and to the President pro tempore of the Senate a report, in writing, setting forth—

the circumstances necessitating the introduction of United States Armed Forces;
the constitutional and legislative authority under which such introduction took place; and
the estimated scope and duration of the hostilities or involvement.

Congressional Action

Sec. 5 (b) Within sixty calendar days after a report is submitted or is required to be submitted pursuant to section 4(a)(1) whichever is earlier, the President shall terminate any use of United States Armed Forces with respect to which such report was submitted (or required to be submitted), unless the Congress (1) has declared war or has enacted a specific authorization for such use of United States Armed Forces, (2) has extended by law such sixty-day period, or (3) is physically unable to meet as a result of an armed attack upon the United States. Such sixty-day period shall be extended for not more than an additional thirty days if the President determines and certifies to the Congress in writing that unavoidable military necessity respecting the safety of United States Armed Forces requires the continued use of such armed forces in the course of bringing about a prompt removal of such forces.

6. Unless there has been a declaration of war, what must the president do within 48 hours of committing armed forces to military action? _____

7. Summarize what must happen within sixty days after the president is required to submit a report to Congress. _____

8. Use outside resources to summarize why the War Powers Act is still a controversial measure today.

AMERICAN GOVERNMENT

Name _____

CHAPTER 9 • ACTIVITY 2

Design a Stamp

Read the feature box on page 195 regarding the stamp designs adopted by the US Postal Service (USPS). Also research the criteria used by the Citizens' Stamp Advisory Committee (CSAC) regarding proposed stamps. Then design a postal stamp.

AMERICAN GOVERNMENT

CHAPTER 9 • ACTIVITY 3

Name _____

The Bible and Poverty

Consider what the Bible says about poverty based on the following passages:

- Exod. 22:25
- Lev. 23:22
- Deut. 14:28–29
- Ps. 72:1–4, 12–14
- Prov. 6:6–11; 14:21, 31; 21:13, 17
- Luke 14:12–14
- Gal. 2:10
- 2 Thess. 3:8–13
- 1 Tim. 5:3–10, 16
- James 2:1–7, 15–17

Select five passages to read. Write a brief essay discussing your findings. Later, as you complete Activity 4 (which deals with growing dependence on government programs), consider what the Bible says about poverty.

AMERICAN GOVERNMENT

Name _____

CHAPTER 9 • ACTIVITY 4

Growing Reliance on Government Support

The Heritage Foundation is a conservative public policy institute located in Washington, DC. The following information appeared in one of their publications in 2012. Read this selection and then answer the questions that follow.

The Heritage Foundation's annual *Index of Dependence on Government* for 2012 shows the continuation of an alarming trend: More than one in five—67 million plus—Americans now rely on government assistance in areas including housing, food, health care, and schooling.

"The most recent data indicate government dependency grew by 8.1 percent in 2011," says Bill Beach, director of Heritage's Center for Data Analysis. Beach also notes that the taxpaying population is shrinking, with half of U.S. households not paying federal income taxes.

The economic impact is clear. The government programs analyzed in the *Index* are key factors in the historic budget deficits [which are causing a rapid growth in the national debt] now facing America, and growing dependency inevitably hurts the nation's rate of economic growth.

As the number of Americans who rely on government subsidies increases, so does the threat to the notion of civil society and close-knit communities.

Heritage understands that dependence isn't a bad thing. Traditionally those in need have looked to their neighbors, families, and churches to help them—and those who help others know they will have support if they are ever in need. "This dependence is a natural part of life," Beach says, "and builds strength and character in communities."

Dependence on government has the opposite effect. "With government dependence, a person goes to a bureaucrat and is given aid without any expectation of anything in return," Beach notes. "As a consequence, people don't have an incentive to get off of that aid, and they're not building personal strength or community bonds. The only thing expanding is the power of the state."

Or, as Allen West, R-FL, put it in a guest post for Heritage's blog, *The Foundry*: "The social safety net—in conjunction with generosity from neighborhood groups, churches, charities, and private companies—can help lift Americans out of poverty and toward the path of self-reliance and individual prosperity. However, that 'net' should never turn into a 'hammock.'"

Heritage Foundation, *Heritage MembersNews*, Spring 2012, p. 4.

1. According to this article, what is an alarming trend? _____

2. What is true of half of US households? _____

3. The article contrasts two types of dependence (the second one is dependence on the government). Summarize that information. _____

4. Do you agree or disagree with the analysis of the types of dependence? Explain your answer. _____

5. What does the last sentence of the article mean? _____

(continued on next page)

The chart on the right indicates the percentage of federal money spent on dependence programs from 1962 to until 2010 (shortly before the information on the previous page was published). Dependence programs include federal assistance to individuals in five areas: (1) housing, (2) healthcare and welfare (including Medicare and Medicaid expenditures); (3) retirement benefits (primarily Social Security payments); (4) assistance in higher education (post-high school); and (5) rural and agricultural services.

Answer the questions below by referring to the chart.

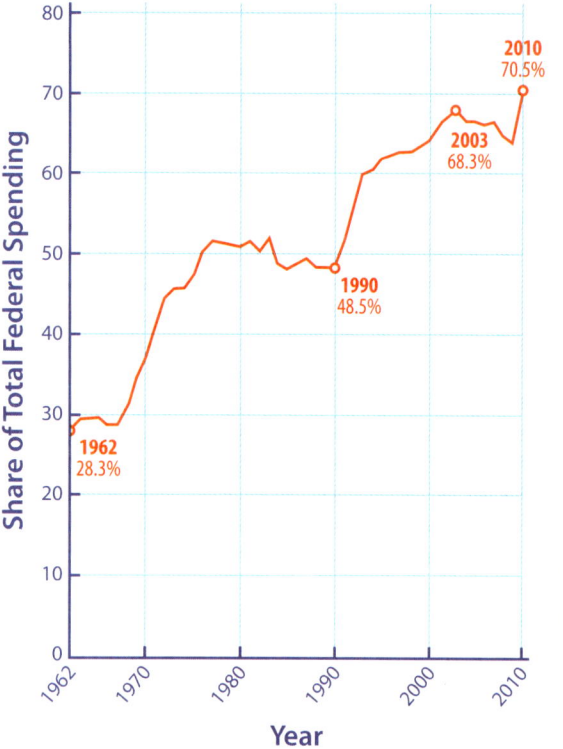

6. In the mid-1960s, President Lyndon Johnson's Great Society programs were enacted. They were intended to eliminate poverty and promote more government involvement in education and health care. How did the enactment of these programs impact federal spending over the next fifteen years? (cite specific statistics)

   _____
   _____
   _____

7. What does the chart indicate about the 1980s?

   _____
   _____
   _____
   _____

8. Explain what occurred between 1990 and 2010 (provide specific statistics). _____
   _____
   _____

9. What *facts* can you state, using the information on the chart, regarding the period from 1962 to 2010? Do not include your opinions. Write only information that can verified by the statistics provided.

   _____
   _____
   _____

10. What is your *opinion* about the information provided? What conclusions do you think can be drawn? How does your essay from Activity 3 (dealing with the Bible and poverty) influence your opinion?

    _____
    _____
    _____
    _____
    _____
    _____

AMERICAN GOVERNMENT

CHAPTER 9 • ACTIVITY 5

Chapter Review

Matching

Match the following terms with their correct definitions or descriptions.

A. duty
B. entitlement
C. excise
D. impeachment
E. implied powers
F. interstate commerce
G. logrolling
H. ratification
I. reprisal
J. subpoena
K. war power

_____ 1. powers that a government has by virtue of being a government

_____ 2. formal charge against the president or other top officials for treason, bribery, or other high crimes and misdemeanors

_____ 3. government compensation programs that are protected by law

_____ 4. a congressman's supporting a colleague's spending project in return for the colleague's supporting his pork-barrel legislation

_____ 5. business transactions between states

_____ 6. a legal order to appear as a witness

_____ 7. a tax on an import

_____ 8. a tax on the production, sale, or use of items and on certain business practices

_____ 9. the formal approval process of a constitution, amendment, or treaty

Short Answer

Read the nonlegislative powers on pages 198–200. Identify nine of the House and the Senate's nonlegislative powers. State which house or houses of Congress have each power.

10–18. _____

_____

_____

_____

_____

_____

_____

(continued on next page)

19. What did the Sixteenth Amendment institute? _____

20. Explain NAFTA. _____
    _____

21. Which clause is the basis for the extraordinary powers of Congress and the national government generally?
    _____

22. What does the Twenty-Fifth Amendment state? _____
    _____
    _____
    _____

Matching

Match the following terms with their correct definitions or descriptions.

A. bankruptcy
B. censure
C. citizenship
D. confirmation
E. enumerated powers
F. letter of marque
G. pork barrel
H. ratification
I. reprimand
J. reprisal
K. reserved powers
L. subpoena
M. war power

_____ 23. belonging to and enjoying all the privileges, rights, and duties as a member of a nation

_____ 24. Senate hearings to accept or reject presidential nominees

_____ 25. declared inability to pay all debts

_____ 26. a license granted by a nation to a private citizen, allowing him to capture merchant ships of another nation

_____ 27. a punishment used only in the House of Representatives, indicating that members are unhappy with the behavior of one of their colleagues

_____ 28. perhaps the single greatest authority given to the national government

_____ 29. political slang for favors obtained for local citizens at the expense of all the taxpayers

_____ 30. a nation's retaliation against another nation when provoked; may involve seizing property or people

_____ 31. powers that are listed in the Constitution

_____ 32. powers kept by the states that enable them to legislate for the health and welfare of their citizens

_____ 33. condemnation by Congress of one of its members whose conduct reflects poorly on the institution

AMERICAN GOVERNMENT

Name _____

CHAPTER 10 • ACTIVITY 1

Choosing Qualified Leaders

Read the following excerpt from No. 64 in *The Federalist Papers.* **That essay was written by John Jay, one of the Founding Fathers. In it, Jay defends the part of the Constitution that grants the president the power to make treaties (which take effect when approved by two-thirds of the Senate). In doing so, he addresses the qualities that leaders should possess. Answer the questions that follow.**

   The second section [Article II, Section 2 of the Constitution] gives power to the President, "BY AND WITH THE ADVICE AND CONSENT OF THE SENATE, TO MAKE TREATIES, PROVIDED TWO THIRDS OF THE SENATORS PRESENT CONCUR."

   The power of making treaties is an important one, especially as it relates to war, peace, and commerce; and it should not be delegated but in such a mode, and with such precautions, as will afford the highest security that it will be exercised by men the best qualified for the purpose, and in the manner most conducive to the public good. The [Constitutional] convention appears to have been attentive to both these points: they have directed the President to be chosen by select bodies of electors [the Electoral College] . . . and they have committed the appointment of senators to the State legislatures [this was true until the adoption of the Seventeenth Amendment in 1913]. . . .

   As the select assemblies [the Electoral College] for choosing the President, as well as the State legislatures who appoint the senators, will in general be composed of the most enlightened and respectable citizens, there is reason to presume that their attention and their votes will be directed to those men only who have become the most distinguished by their abilities and virtue, and in whom the people perceive just grounds for confidence. The Constitution manifests very particular attention to this object. By excluding men under thirty-five from the first office [the presidency], and those under thirty from the second [the Senate], it confines the electors to men of whom the people have had time to form a judgment. . . .

1. What are Jay's primary assumptions in his argument about the qualities of those who would become president and senators? Do you think his assumptions have been proven true? Why or why not?

   _____
   _____
   _____
   _____
   _____

2. What are the age requirements for the president and senators? _____
   _____

3. Do you think that Jay was correct in his assumption that having the age requirement of thirty-five would ensure that only the best candidates would be elected president? Why or why not? _____
   _____
   _____
   _____

(continued on next page)

The inference which naturally results from these considerations is this, that the President and senators so chosen will always be of the number of those who best understand our national interests, whether considered in relation to the several States or to foreign nations, who are best able to promote those interests, and whose reputation for integrity inspires and merits confidence. With such men the power of making treaties may be safely lodged.

4. Jay implies that men who met the qualifications he set down would always have the nation's best interests at heart. Has this always been the case with American presidents? Why or why not? _____
_____
_____
_____
_____
_____

5. Read the quotation from John Adams, our second president, on the opening page of Chapter 11 of the student text. Do you think Adams agreed with Jay's optimistic attitude toward those who would become president? Why? _____
_____
_____
_____

6. Although the Constitution stipulates only three broad requirements for president, what other qualities do you think are critical to consider in anyone who would be president? _____
_____
_____
_____
_____

AMERICAN GOVERNMENT

Name _____

CHAPTER 10 • ACTIVITY 2

A Brokered Convention: The Democratic National Convention, 1924

Read the following description of the 1924 Democratic National Convention. Then answer the questions that follow.

Today, the nominating process at each party's national convention is relatively simple when compared with the process that was in place in 1924. In the past few decades, the nominees of each party have generally had their nominations "in the bag" before they even arrived at the convention. This is partly because many candidates withdraw during the presidential primary season after failing to achieve as many votes as they had hoped. Thus, the front-runner often faces little serious opposition from other candidates at the convention. Such was definitely *not* the case at the 1924 Democratic National Convention.

The convention opened in Madison Square Garden in New York City on June 24, 1924. It did not produce a nominee until July 9 after a record 103 ballots were cast. The party entered the convention with only two serious candidates: Alfred E. Smith, the governor of New York, and William McAdoo, the treasury secretary under President Woodrow Wilson. But neither of them had the required two-thirds support of the more than one thousand delegates. On the first ballot, seventeen other candidates split the vote with McAdoo and Smith. Most of those candidates were not serious contenders but rather were "favorite sons." This term refers to candidates nominated by delegates from their home states as an honor, and with the hope that a major candidate would offer them some political favor in return for their agreement to withdraw and support that major candidate. However, in 1924, most favorite sons remained in the race. On the one hundredth ballot, seventeen candidates were still in the contest.

McAdoo received the most votes on the first ballot and throughout most of the voting. By the eighty-sixth ballot, however, he had slipped to second; Smith took the lead and a dark horse (a little-known candidate), John W. Davis, had climbed to third place. But none of those three had anywhere near the two-thirds support necessary to win. Part of the problem with selecting a nominee was that key issues divided the party and the leading candidates. First, McAdoo was a Prohibitionist, a "dry," but Smith was anti-Prohibition, a "wet." Second, the Ku Klux Klan supported McAdoo, whereas it opposed Smith, who was a Roman Catholic. Those on both sides of the issues felt so strongly about their respective positions that neither side would waver.

1. Why are political conventions now much simpler than they were a century ago? _____
   _____

2. How many ballots were required for the delegates at the 1924 Democratic convention to select a nominee? _____
   _____

3. How long did the convention last? _____

4. What is a favorite son? _____
   _____

5. What is a dark horse candidate? _____

6. What problems made selecting a nominee so difficult for Democrats in 1924? _____
   _____
   _____

(continued on next page)

Finally, however, after sixteen grueling days of balloting, the convention nominated John W. Davis. In the November election, Davis was easily defeated by the Republican candidate, incumbent president Calvin Coolidge.

Other brokered conventions (a convention that requires multiple ballots and eventual settlement by bargaining and compromise) followed; however, none were as long as that of Democratic convention of 1924. In 1932 the Democrats required four ballots to choose Franklin Roosevelt over Al Smith and James Nance Garner. However, at the 1936 Democratic convention, the party abolished the century-old rule that a candidate must receive a two-thirds vote of the delegates to become the nominee. The new requirement was that a candidate must simply receive a majority of the delegate votes. Though the rule change greatly diminished the likelihood of a brokered convention, Democrats still narrowly escaped such a convention in 1948. That year Southern "Dixiecrats" walked out of the convention and nominated Strom Thurmond to run on the States' Rights ticket while the remainder of the convention nominated Harry Truman over Richard Russell.

Republicans never required a two-thirds vote for a candidate to become the party's nominee. However, in 1948, their convention still struggled through three ballots before choosing Thomas Dewey over a crowded field that included General Douglas MacArthur. The last brokered convention occurred at the Democratic convention in 1952, when it took three ballots to select Adlai Stevenson over rivals that included Estes Kefauver and Richard Russell.

Brokered conventions are usually very detrimental to political parties. After a divisive convention, it is often difficult to convince party members to unify in support of the eventual nominee. The last time a brokered convention produced a presidency-winning candidate was 1932. That was the year that Democrat Franklin Roosevelt was elected.

7. Who was eventually selected by convention delegates to be the Democrats' nominee in 1924? _____

8. What is a brokered convention? _____

9. What change was made at the 1936 Democratic convention? Why was this significant? _____

10. What rule did the Republican Party never institute regarding the party's nomination? _____

11. Describe the last brokered convention that occurred. _____

12. Why are brokered conventions detrimental to political parties? _____

13. Explain the significance of the 1932 election. _____

14. Do you think a brokered convention could occur today? _____

AMERICAN GOVERNMENT

Name _____

CHAPTER 10 • ACTIVITY 3

Presidential Debates

Using outside resources, compare the 1960 presidential debates with the famous Lincoln-Douglas debates in the 1858 Illinois senatorial race. Describe such factors as those listed in the following table, but also add others that you think are important.

Factor	Lincoln-Douglas debates	1960 presidential debates
Number of debates		
Location of debates		
Length of debates		
Number and names of participants		
Format followed		
How reported		
Other important factors or items of interest		

83

AMERICAN GOVERNMENT

CHAPTER 10 • ACTIVITY 4

The Disputed Election of 1876

After Ulysses S. Grant's two presidential terms, the 1876 election pitted Republican Rutherford B. Hayes against Democrat Samuel Tilden. Read the following excerpts from a book about that election written by the late Supreme Court chief justice William Rehnquist. It details how the disputed election was resolved. Answer the questions that follow.

People were prepared for a close vote, but scarcely anyone guessed just how close it would be. . . .

All of the New England states except Connecticut . . . were carried by Hayes, but by considerably smaller margins than Grant's in 1872. Connecticut . . . went even more narrowly for Tilden. . . .

Tilden carried his home state [New York] by a margin of some 30,000 votes, and neighboring New Jersey by a similar margin. . . . Pennsylvania remained narrowly Republican, but Delaware switched. South of the Mason-Dixon line, the only Republican hopes were in Florida, South Carolina, and Louisiana, where President Grant had sent troops the preceding day. . . .

Of the [southern] states which were in dispute [Florida, South Carolina, and Louisiana], Florida was most different in 1876 from what it is today [2004, when this book was published]. . . . There were slightly fewer than 50,000 votes cast in the 1876 presidential election [in Florida], in contrast with the more than 6 million counted in 2000. . . .

On the face of the returns from the various [Florida] counties, Tilden led Hayes, but by a margin of only 80-some votes. The [state election] board exercised its discretion to reject some of these returns. . . . It finally concluded that Hayes had won the state over Tilden by a majority of 45 votes.

In Louisiana, the returns from throughout the state on their face gave Tilden a lead of between 8,000 and 9,000. . . . [But the state election board] rejected more than 13,000 Democratic and about 2,500 Republican ballots. The result gave Hayes a majority of a little more than 3,000, which was certified and sent to Washington. . . .

In South Carolina, federal troops had been stationed in various parts of the state ever since the end of the Civil War. . . . On election day, there was illegal voting by both white Democrats and black Republicans. The Democrats carried their state ticket [electing their candidate as governor] . . . but the same ballots gave Hayes a win over Tilden. The Board of Canvassers [i.e., state election board] so certified the results . . . [in spite of] the efforts of the state supreme court to thwart it.

1. Name the two presidential candidates and their parties in the election of 1876 (see introductory information). _____

2. Which three southern states' votes were at the center of the controversy in the election? _____

3. Explain the controversies that emerged regarding the results in the three southern states noted above.
_____
_____
_____
_____
_____

(continued on next page)

[In Congress, each chamber] appointed committees to investigate the vote counts in contested states. The House named a special committee and directed its members to go to Florida, Louisiana, and South Carolina to conduct its inquiries. One day later, the Senate Commission on Privileges and Elections was charged with a similar mission. . . .

The respective committees . . . took voluminous testimony from a great number of witnesses. . . . The majority of the Senate committee—all Republicans—reported that the electoral votes of Louisiana, Florida, and South Carolina belonged to Hayes. The minority—all Democrats—concluded that they belonged to Tilden. In the House, the . . . reports were the exact opposite of those in the Senate. The two houses were at loggerheads; there was no evident way that Congress, following its regular procedures, could resolve the election.

The House committee then recommended that the five senior justices of the Supreme Court—Nathan Clifford and Stephen Field, thought to be sympathetic to the Democrats, Samuel Miller and Noah Swayne, thought to be sympathetic to the Republicans, and David Davis, who was regarded as an Independent—should be named to [a special Electoral Commission in order to settle the dispute. The Commission also included five Senate members, and five House members. Of those fifteen members, eight were Republicans and seven were Democrats. These members were to determine how to resolve the dispute regarding the nineteen electoral votes of Florida, Louisiana, and South Carolina, as well as a disputed electoral vote from Oregon.]

The decision of the Commission was to be final, unless overridden by a majority in each house.

. . . Hayes needed every one of the [twenty] disputed votes in order to win; if Tilden could win only one of them, he would be President.

[The end result was that the Commission awarded all twenty of the disputed votes to Hayes] by a vote of 8 to 7—all of the Republicans voting for it and all of the Democrats voting against it. [There were not enough Democrats in Congress to overrule the decision. The addition of the disputed votes gave Hayes 185 electoral votes to Tilden's 184. Thus, Hayes became president.]

Excerpt(s) from CENTENNIAL CRISIS: THE DISPUTED ELECTION OF 1876 by William H. Rehnquist, copyright © 2004 by William H. Rehnquist. Used by permission of Alfred A. Knopf, an imprint of the Knopf Doubleday Publishing Group, a division of Penguin Random House LLC. All rights reserved.

4. Eventually a commission was appointed to settle the dispute. How many members served in this body, and what parts of the government did they represent? _____

5. Explain how the Commission settled the dispute. _____

6. Why do you think many people questioned the conclusion of the Commission? _____

7. Read the feature box on page 238 about the presidential election of 2000. What are some parallels between that disputed election and the one in 1876? _____

AMERICAN GOVERNMENT

Name _____

CHAPTER 10 • ACTIVITY 5

Chapter Review

Answer the following questions.

1. What are the three qualifications that the Constitution establishes for the president? _____

2. What is the name for the preliminary nominating elections that are held to select candidates or to select delegates to party conventions? _____

3. Define *caucus*. _____

4. What are the two basic purposes of the presidential primary? _____

5. Define *closed primaries*. _____

6. Define *open primaries*. _____

7. Define *crossover voting*. _____

8. Describe *raiding*. _____

9. Which state has the first presidential caucuses? _____

10. Which state has the first presidential primary? _____

11. Define *party platform*. _____

12. What term is used for party leaders and officeholders who serve as uncommitted delegates to the Democratic national convention? _____

13. What name is given to a speech usually made on the opening day of a party's national convention by a leading party member? _____

(continued on next page)

14. Define *brokered convention*. _____
    _____
    _____

15. What phrase refers to a presidential candidate's choosing a running mate who can strengthen his chance of being elected due to specific ideology, geography, race, gender, or other characteristics? _____
    _____

16. When is the general election for president held? _____
    _____

17. Which state figured most prominently in the disputed presidential election of 2000? _____

18. Which presidential candidates were involved in the first televised debates? _____
    _____

19. What do the media use on Election Day to predict an election's outcome before a final tally is completed?
    _____

20. Why is the Electoral College considered a safeguard? _____
    _____
    _____

21. Identify the last two presidential elections (and the candidates) in which the person elected president did not win the popular vote. _____
    _____

22. When does the Electoral College meet? _____

23. What is the name for the office in which the president conducts business? _____

24. What is the term for the president's release of a convicted person from the remainder of his or her sentence? _____

25. When is Inauguration Day? _____

AMERICAN GOVERNMENT

CHAPTER 11 • ACTIVITY 1

President vs. King

In essay No. 69 of *The Federalist Papers*, Alexander Hamilton compares the office of the president of the United States with that of the British king. Read the following excerpt. Identify the differences between the two by completing the table below and on the following page.

   The President of the United States would be an officer elected by the people for *four* years; the king of Great Britain is a perpetual and *hereditary* prince. The one would be amenable [subject] to personal punishment and disgrace; the person of the other is sacred and inviolable [viewed with reverence]. The one would have a *qualified* negative upon the acts of the legislative body; the other has an *absolute* negative. The one would have a right to command the military and naval forces of the nation; the other, in addition to this right, possesses that of *declaring* war, and of *raising* and *regulating* fleets and armies by his own authority. The one would have a concurrent [joint] power with a branch of the legislature [the Senate] in the formation of treaties; the other is the *sole possessor* of the power of making treaties. The one would have a like concurrent authority in appointing to offices; the other is the sole author of all appointments. The one can confer no privileges whatever; the other can make denizens [citizens] of aliens, noblemen of commoners; can erect corporations with all the rights incident to corporate bodies. The one can prescribe no rules concerning the commerce or currency of the nation; the other . . . can establish markets and fairs, can regulate weights and measures, can lay embargoes for a limited time, can coin money, can authorize or prohibit the circulation of foreign coin. The one has no particle of spiritual jurisdiction [control]; the other is the supreme head and governor of the national church! What answer shall we give to those who would persuade us that things so unlike resemble each other? The same that ought to be given to those who tell us that a government, the whole power of which would be in the hands of the elective and periodical servants of the people, is an aristocracy, a monarchy, and a despotism.

Characteristics	President	King
1. Origin of leadership (method of selection)		
2. Length of service		
3. Accountability		
4. Ability to stop legislation (veto power)		

(continued on next page)

Characteristics	President	King
5. Command of military and naval forces		
6. Declaring war		
7. Raising and regulating military and naval forces		
8. Making treaties		
9. Making office appointments		
10. Conferring privileges		
11. Make laws concerning commerce or currency		
12. Spiritual jurisdiction		

AMERICAN GOVERNMENT

Name _____

CHAPTER 11 • ACTIVITY 2

The Proper Attitude Toward the Powers of the Presidency

Read the following excerpts from a speech by Mike Pence. At the time it was delivered to students and faculty at Hillsdale College, he was a US representative from Indiana. He later served as governor of the state and was then elected as the nation's vice president in 2016. Answer the questions that follow.

   The powers of the presidency are extraordinary and necessarily great, and great presidents treat them sparingly. For example, it is not the president's job to manipulate the nation's youth for the sake of his agenda or his party. They are a potent political force when massed by the social network to which they are permanently attached. But if the president has their true interests at heart he will neither flatter them nor let them adore him, for in flattery is condescension and in adoration is direction, and youth is neither seasoned nor tested enough to direct a nation. Nor should it be the president's business to presume to direct them. It is difficult enough to do right by one's own children. No one can be the father of a whole continent's youth.

   Is the president, therefore, expected to turn away from this and other easy advantage? Yes. Like Harry Truman, who went to bed before the result on election night, he must know when to withdraw, to hold back, and to forgo attention, publicity, or advantage.

   There is no finer, more moving, or more profound understanding of the nature of the presidency and the command of humility placed upon it than that expressed by President Coolidge. He, like Lincoln, lost a child while he was president, a son of sixteen. "The day I became president," Coolidge wrote, "he had just started to work in a tobacco field. When one of his fellow laborers said to him, 'If my father was president I would not work in a tobacco field,' Calvin replied, 'If my father were your father you would.'" His admiration for the boy was obvious.

   Young Calvin contracted blood poisoning from an incident on the South Lawn of the White House. Coolidge wrote, "What might have happened to him under other circumstances we do not know, but if I had not been president. . . ." And then he continued, "In his suffering he was asking me to make him well. I could not. When he went, the power and glory of the presidency went with him."

1. How does Pence say great presidents treat the powers of the presidency? _____

2. Pence states some ways he thinks a president should deal with the nation's youth. Explain those.
   _____
   _____
   _____
   _____

3. What lesson did you think Pence is presenting by telling the story of Coolidge's son working in a tobacco field? _____
   _____

4. What incident during Coolidge's presidency taught him humility and a proper view of his power as president? _____
   _____

(continued on next page)

A sensibility such as this, and not power, is the source of presidential dignity, and must be restored. It depends entirely upon character, self-discipline, and an understanding of the fundamental principles that underlie not only the republic, but life itself. It communicates that the president feels the gravity of his office and is willing to sacrifice himself; that his eye is not upon his own prospects but on the storm of history, through which he must navigate with the specific powers accorded to him and the limitations placed on those powers both by man and by God. . . .

[A]lthough we may have strayed [from the Founders' principles], we have not strayed too far to return. . . . We can still astound the world with justice, reason and strength. I know this is true, but even if it was not we could not in decency stand down, if only for our debt to history. We owe a debt to those who came before, who did great things, and suffered more than we suffer, and gave more than we give, and pledged their lives, their fortunes, and their sacred honor for us, whom they did not know. For we "drink from wells we did not dig" and are "warmed by fires we did not build," and so we must be faithful in our time as they were in theirs.

Many great generations are gone, but by the character and memory of their existence they forbid us to despair of the republic. I see them crossing the prairies in the sun and wind. I see their faces looking out from steel mills and coal mines, and immigrant ships crawling into the harbors at dawn. I see them at war, at work, and at peace. I see them, long departed, looking into the camera, with hopeful and sad eyes. And I see them embracing their children, who became us. They are our family and our blood, and we cannot desert them. In spirit, all of them come down to all of us, in a connection that, out of love, we cannot betray.

They are silent now and forever, but from the eternal silence of every patriot grave there is yet an echo that says, "It is not too late; keep faith with us, keep faith with God, and do not, do not ever despair of the republic."

From Mike Pence, "The Presidency and the Constitution," *Imprimis*, vol. 39, no. 10 (October 2010). Reprinted by permission from Imprimis, a publication of Hillsdale College.

5. According to Pence, on what three factors does a restoration of presidential dignity depend?

6. What does Pence mean when he says that we "drink from wells we did not dig" and we are "warmed by fires we did not build"?

7. Does Pence have a generally positive or a negative view regarding the American republic's future? Why?

8. Do you agree or disagree with Pence's assessment? Defend your answer.

AMERICAN GOVERNMENT

Name _____

CHAPTER 11 • ACTIVITY 3

Comparing First Ladies

Choose a First Lady from each of the following time periods. Use additional resources to complete the chart with the appropriate information and answer the discussion question.

	1789–1860	1861–1945	1946–Present
First Lady			
Date and place of birth			
Education			
Interesting fact(s) about her life prior to entering the White House			
Personality description			
Contributions and/or interests while serving as First Lady			

Discussion: Which of these three First Ladies do you think made the most positive contribution to the position of First Lady? Why? _____

_____

_____

_____

_____

AMERICAN GOVERNMENT

CHAPTER 11 • ACTIVITY 4

John Nance Garner on the Vice Presidency

Read the following account of John Nance Garner's experiences as vice president. He served during the first eight years that Franklin Roosevelt was president. Answer the questions that follow.

Garner never pretended to enjoy his new job [as vice president], and it is doubtful if any other Vice President so consistently maligned [criticized, denounced] the office. "A great man may be Vice-President," said Garner, "but he can't be a great Vice-President, because the office in itself is unimportant." Some of his other remarks were less eloquent. . . .

During their first term Roosevelt and Garner established what seemed to be a model working relationship. Once again, a Vice President attended Cabinet meetings. Garner became the first Vice President to travel abroad in an official capacity, when he attended the installation of Manuel Quezon as President of the Republic of the Philippines in 1935. The next year he persuaded Roosevelt to establish weekly legislative conferences with Congressional leaders, in which Garner also participated.

At the Cabinet meetings, Garner endeavored to explain the mysteries of Congress to Roosevelt and to his [the president's] band of professorial brain trusters and other political amateurs. Garner's report on conditions there was sometimes gloomy and betrayed his own wish that he had remained as Speaker. In 1934 he told the Cabinet that he had never seen the House of Representatives in such turmoil. Garner criticized the House leaders who, he said, seemed to have no control over the House and little apparent disposition to get behind Administration legislation.

As long as Garner enjoyed the confidence of both the executive and legislative branches, he could serve very effectively in a liaison role. . . .

1. How could you summarize Garner's assessment of the vice presidency? _____
   _____

2. In what ways did Garner try to use the office of vice president to help the Roosevelt administration?
   _____
   _____

But Garner's position was fraught with possibilities for mischief should he have a falling-out with Roosevelt. . . . As late as 1935, the Vice President told Interior Secretary Harold Ickes that he felt that the Administration had not gone far enough to satisfy the expectations of the public for a liberal government. . . .

On the other hand, . . . [a]s the 1930's progressed, and as the country showed signs of climbing out of the depression, Garner gradually concluded that he could best serve his country by restraining the President. . . .

Like Thomas R. Marshall [Woodrow Wilson's vice president], Garner expected that his second four years would be a breeze. Roosevelt said that he would never again run for public office, and Garner vowed that he wouldn't either. The President, however, saw the 1936 landslide as a call for more liberal legislation. From time to time at Cabinet meetings, Garner would interject the admonition, "Mr. President, you know you've got to let the cattle graze."

3. What contradictory views did Garner have concerning FDR? _____
   _____
   _____

(continued on next page)

FDR's proposed reform of the Federal judiciary—his court-packing bill—brought the Democratic party to the crossroads in the summer of 1937. [For each US Supreme Court justice over age seventy that did not retire, FDR wanted to appoint an additional justice up to a maximum of six. Such action would ensure that his supporters controlled the court.] . . .

Instead of consulting with the legislative branch on this most important and controversial bill, Roosevelt called in Congressional leaders—including Garner—and unveiled down to the last comma the heretofore secret bill that he wished passed. Garner was stunned by this procedure. . . .

. . . Many Congressmen who disagreed with some of the Court's decisions were opposed to a move that threatened to undermine the independence of the judiciary. Garner himself, in the Senate lobby, held his nose and gave a thumbs-down sign, perhaps his first open display of contempt for a position taken by the President.

In June, with the Senate about to vote on the Court bill, Garner [who, as Vice President, served as the president of the Senate] and his wife left Washington for a Texas vacation they had planned five months before. Roosevelt was annoyed at what he regarded as a walkout by the Vice President. . . .

On July 14, Majority Leader Robinson dropped dead of a heart attack brought on by his struggle to save Roosevelt's Court bill. With Robinson dead, support for the measure melted away. When Garner returned to Washington and told Roosevelt that he was beaten, the President asked the Vice President to arrange the best possible compromise. It is not clear to what extent Garner attempted to salvage any part of the wreckage, but the record shows that the Senate voted to return the bill to committee, in effect killing it. . . .

4. Describe Garner's actions regarding FDR's plan to enlarge the US Supreme Court. _____
_____
_____
_____

The culmination of the ideological and personal estrangement between Roosevelt and Garner came in the summer of 1940, when the President stood as a candidate for a third term. The Vice President strenuously opposed a third term, arguing: "A President, any President, weak or strong, is in position to exercise great power from the first breath he draws after taking office until he leaves that office. No man should exercise the great powers of the Presidency too long." And he said on another occasion: "I would be against a third term on principle even if I approved every act of Roosevelt's two terms. I would oppose my own brother for a third term."

Garner left Washington forever in 1941 [as FDR began his third term and Henry Wallace became the new Vice President], filled with deep unhappiness, distrust of Roosevelt and his policies, and concern for the welfare of the country.

Donald Young, *American Roulette: The History and Dilemma of the Vice Presidency.* N.Y.: Holt, Rinehart and Winston, 1965 (pp. 167–70, 172–73).

5. Discuss Garner's view of FDR's desire for, and election to, a third term. _____
_____
_____

6. Do you agree or disagree with Garner's assessment that the vice presidency was an unimportant office and that a great man cannot be a great vice president? Defend your position on each issue. _____
_____
_____
_____
_____

AMERICAN GOVERNMENT

Name _____

CHAPTER 11 • ACTIVITY 5

Comparing Presidents

Choose a president from each of the following time periods. Use additional resources to complete the chart with the appropriate information and answer the discussion question.

	1789–1860	*1861–1945*	*1946–Present*
President			
Date and place of birth			
Education			
Occupation prior to presidency			
Major domestic policy issues			
Major foreign policy issues			

Discussion: Which of these three presidents do you think was the most successful in his domestic policies? Why?

_____
_____
_____
_____
_____

AMERICAN GOVERNMENT

Name _____

CHAPTER 11 • ACTIVITY 6

Chapter Review

Matching

Match the following terms with their correct definitions or descriptions.

A. cabinet
B. covert operations
C. executive agreement
D. executive orders
E. extradition
F. impeachment
G. lame duck
H. line-item veto
I. pocket veto
J. quorum
K. state dinner
L. State of the Union
M. suffrage
N. tenure
O. veto

_____ 1. occurs when the president leaves a bill unsigned for ten days and Congress has adjourned

_____ 2. hosted by the president and First Lady to honor a visiting foreign leader

_____ 3. bringing charges against the president or another major government official

_____ 4. activities approved by the president that are unknown to the public (and sometimes to Congress)

_____ 5. means "term of office"

_____ 6. can be overridden by a two-thirds vote of both houses of Congress

_____ 7. group of high ranking officials that assist the president in his constitutional duties

_____ 8. a written understanding between the president and another head of state

_____ 9. presidential power approved by Congress but later ruled as unconstitutional by the Supreme Court

_____ 10. used to describe a president who has lost an election or is ineligible for reelection

_____ 11. presidential directives that have the force of law

_____ 12. provided by the president to Congress to report the condition of the country

Short Answer

Write the appropriate answers in the spaces provided.

13. Effective 2001, what is the president's annual salary? _____

14. What is the name of the airplane that transports the president? _____

15. What is the name for the helicopter that transports the president? _____

16. After the president signs a treaty, what must be done in order for it to be approved? _____

(continued on next page)

17. What is the CIA and its mission? _____
    _____

18. What is the name for the presidential retreat in Maryland? _____

19. Which amendment established limits regarding the number of years the president can serve?
    _____

20. Today, what is the maximum number of terms to which the president can be elected? _____

21. Today, what is the maximum number of years a president can serve? _____

22. After a president is impeached, what must occur before he can be removed from office? ___
    _____

23. What does the Twenty-Fifth Amendment state? _____
    _____
    _____

24. Who would become president if both the president and vice president died? _____

25. What is the NSC, and what are its responsibilities? _____
    _____

26. What is the OMB, and what are its responsibilities? _____
    _____

27. Today, how many cabinet offices exist? _____

Matching

Match each president with the correct description.

A. Bill Clinton   D. Abraham Lincoln   G. Franklin Roosevelt
B. Gerald Ford   E. William McKinley   H. Theodore Roosevelt
C. Andrew Johnson   F. Richard Nixon

_____ 28. resigned from the presidency

_____ 29. his death prompted Congress to ask the Secret Service to provide protection for presidents

_____ 30. elected president four times

_____ 31. first president to be impeached

_____ 32. second president to be impeached

_____ 33. appointed vice president to fill a vacancy there

AMERICAN GOVERNMENT

CHAPTER 12 • ACTIVITY 1

The Case for Bureaucracy

By Paul R. Verkuil
Oct. 3, 2016, *The New York Times*

Below are excerpts from an editorial that was written during the 2016 presidential campaign. The following month, Donald Trump defeated Hillary Clinton. Read this selection and then answer the questions that follow.

   In a recent speech, Donald J. Trump revived a Republican plan to reduce the federal work force in part by replacing only some of the employees who retire . . . He also said he wanted to raise money by eliminating waste, collecting unpaid taxes and stopping improper tax payments.
   But these two goals—decreasing the federal work force and avoiding government excess and mismanagement—are actually contradictory, despite all the political rhetoric about the perils of bureaucracy. . . .
   I spent the last five years serving as chairman of the Administrative Conference of the United States, a bipartisan federal agency established in 1964 whose mission is to improve government processes and performance. My experience there taught me that we need more professionals in government, not fewer; they would both improve government performance and save money.
   The Internal Revenue Service, for example, offers a compelling case for adding professionals. Mr. Trump talks about raising revenue by collecting unpaid taxes, and according to the I.R.S., the "tax gap" of unpaid but owed taxes is some $400 billion. If only 20 percent of that could be collected, it would yield substantial funds. But we need agents to collect these owed taxes and to perform audits. Historically, I.R.S. employees have returned many times the dollar amount invested in their salaries and benefits. The audit rate is now at a record low, however, and the I.R.S. relies increasingly on a tradition of voluntary taxpayer compliance, which is waning. . . .
   Moreover, another of Mr. Trump's proposed revenue sources, stopping improper payments, would also be aided by more I.R.S. agents. The Government Accountability Office has shown that billions of dollars are paid to those who hack into taxpayers' accounts and divert refunds. Existing staff members simply can't keep up with these technologically sophisticated perpetrators of fraud. More professionals, schooled in cybersecurity, are called for.

1. According to the author, what two goals are contradictory? _____
   _____

2. What two reasons does the author give for supporting the hiring of more professionals in government?
   _____

3. Summarize the illustration given regarding the collection of unpaid taxes. _____
   _____
   _____
   _____

(continued on next page)

There is a common misconception that our bureaucracy has grown out of control. The federal civilian work force (excepting Postal Service employees) is about two million, roughly the same size it was during the Kennedy administration. In effect, the Civil Service has drastically shrunk since then, for the gross domestic product has multiplied five times, and numerous new agencies (like the Environmental Protection Agency and the Department of Homeland Security) have added significant and complicated missions to the federal agenda.

Because of a shortage of federal positions, the only way these agencies could be staffed was by adding contractors, who, according to one estimate, now exceed the number of federal workers by a factor of four. These contractors . . . are often more costly than a government counterpart would be. . . .

4. The author mentions what he calls a common misconception. Explain his position. _____

There are so many horror stories about our dreaded bureaucracy that the idea of maintaining or even increasing it may seem odd or quixotic, but the case is clear. What we really need are Civil Service reforms to make it easier to hire qualified people to run the complex missions of our government, and fire those who don't measure up. . . .

Increase the professionals in government and you'll get better government, while at the same time finding some of the funds you need for other purposes.

From The New York Times, Oct. 3, 2016 © 2016 The New York Times. All rights reserved. Used by permission and protected by the Copyright Laws of the United States. The printing, copying, redistribution, or retransmission of this Content without express written permission is prohibited.

5. What two things does the author say civil service reforms are needed to accomplish? _____

6. Restate the author's conclusions. _____

7. Do you agree or disagree with the arguments presented in this article? _____

AMERICAN GOVERNMENT

Name _____

CHAPTER 12 • ACTIVITY 2

The Cabinet

Use outside sources to identify the head of each cabinet department. Then choose one cabinet member and research that person's life. Write a biographical sketch of that individual on the reverse side.

Department of State _____

Department of the Treasury _____

Department of Defense _____

Department of Justice _____

Department of the Interior _____

Department of Agriculture _____

Department of Commerce _____

Department of Labor _____

Department of Health and Human Services _____

Department of Housing and Urban Development _____

Department of Transportation _____

Department of Energy _____

Department of Education _____

Department of Veterans Affairs _____

Department of Homeland Security _____

Selected cabinet secretary _____

(continued on next page)

Biographical Sketch

AMERICAN GOVERNMENT

CHAPTER 12 • ACTIVITY 3

Name _____

Is Administrative Law Constitutional?

Philip Hamburger is a professor of law at Columbia Law School. He has argued in several books that administrative law, rules and regulations devised by the government's bureaucracy, is actually unlawful. Read the following excerpt from his writings and answer the questions.

Over the past century, most complaints about administrative power [administrative law] have come from an economic perspective. It is said that administrative power is inefficient, dangerously centralized, burdensome on business, destructive of jobs, and stifling for innovation and growth. All of this is painfully true, but these are largely economic complaints, and economic complaints are not the entire critique of administrative power....

For a better understanding of the administrative threat, one must turn to law. The legal critique more fully addresses the problem than does the economic protest, for although much administrative power is economically inefficient, all of it is unconstitutional....

This is not to deny that [legitimate] executive power is extensive. Executive power is often portrayed as merely the power to execute the laws, but more accurately (as recognized by Alexander Hamilton) it amounts to the power to execute all of the nation's lawful force. It thus includes the power to prosecute offenders in court, to exercise discretion in distributing benefits, to determine the status of immigrants, and so forth....

1. List the ways that administrative laws are harmful from an economic perspective. _____
   _____
   _____

2. The article gives three examples of powers that the bureaucracy can exercise. Identify these.
   _____
   _____

[Administrative power] ... binds Americans and deprives them of their liberty, not through acts of Congress and acts of the courts but through other mechanisms. And this evasion of the Constitution's pathways for law is what makes the legal objection to administrative power so central....

[The Constitution] authorizes only two pathways for government to bind Americans, in the sense of imposing legal obligations on them. Although a few exceptions will be noted later, the government generally can impose binding rules only through acts of Congress (or treaties ratified by the Senate), and can impose binding adjudications [decisions] only through acts of the courts. These are its lawful options....

3. According to the article, what does administrative power do to Americans? _____
   _____

4. Summarize what the Constitution authorizes, according to the author, regarding imposing legal obligations on Americans. _____
   _____
   _____

(continued on next page)

Administrative [bureaucratic] lawmaking is often justified as delegated power—as if Congress could divest itself of the power that the people had delegated to it. The Constitution, however, expressly bars any such subdelegation....

[The Constitution says:] "All legislative powers herein granted shall be vested in a Congress...." If all legislative powers are to be in Congress, they cannot be elsewhere. If the grant were merely permissive, not exclusive, there would be no reason for the word All. That word bars subdelegation....

The Fifth Amendment guarantees "the due process of law" and thereby bars the government from working outside the courts to issue orders to particular persons....

There was once a constitutional right to the full due process of law in the courts of law for binding adjudications [decisions]—adjudications that impose legal obligations—whether in cutting off life or restricting liberty or property. This essential right, however, has been reduced to a mere administrative "hearing" (often where one cannot be heard) and more typically "something less."

The familiar result is that federal agencies can demand testimony and private records and can impose fines without even going to court, let alone offering much administrative process.

5. Summarize what the author says about legislative powers. _____

6. Explain what the author believes regarding "due process of law" and how he believes bureaucratic power deprives individuals of it. _____

Although administrative power is the nation's preeminent [predominate] threat to civil liberties, many commentators worry that the nation cannot get along without it. In fact, the resulting economic problems suggest that the nation cannot afford to retain administrative power. But even so, it remains to be considered whether government is practicable without it.

For example, is administrative power the only means of rapid legislative change? Actually, when Congress wishes, it can act faster than most agencies, while relying on their expertise. Popular complaints about congressional "gridlock" therefore do not usually reflect the realities....

How much ... involves genuine emergencies—matters that simply cannot wait for Congress to act? ... Most claims of emergencies are merely excuses to shift power out of Congress....

Americans therefore need to recognize that administrative power revives absolute power and profoundly threatens civil liberties. Once Americans understand this, they can begin to push back, and the fate of administrative power will then be only a matter of time.

Hamburger, Philip, *The Administrative Threat*, New York: Encounter Books, 2017, pp. 1–3, 22–24, 30–32, 57–58, 64.

7. Those who defend administrative power often say it is necessary in order to handle matters in a timely or prompt manner. Explain this argument and the author's answer to it. _____

8. How does the author conclude this argument? Do you agree or disagree with his assessment? Explain your answer. _____

Bureaucracy Cartoon

Draw a political cartoon focusing on the government bureaucracy. It might highlight problems, such as red tape, duplication, or waste, or it may present a positive view of a government agency or program. On the reverse side, explain your cartoon.

(continued on next page)

Cartoon Explanation

AMERICAN GOVERNMENT

Name _____

CHAPTER 12 • ACTIVITY 5

Chapter Review

Answer the following questions.

1. Define *bureaucracy*. _____
   _____

2. Define *bureaucrat*. _____

3. Identify the principle of delegation. _____

4. What is the civil service? _____

5. What legislation, adopted in 1883, established the Civil Service Commission? _____

6. What new standard for hiring and promoting civil employees was established by that 1883 law? _____

7. Who advises the president on issues of politics, policy, and management? _____

8. Who is the official spokesperson for the president? _____

9. Which agency is the president's policymaking group over security and intelligence matters? _____
   _____

10. Define *cabinet*. _____
    _____

11. How many cabinet-level departments are in the executive branch? _____

12. What is statutory law? _____

13. Define *administrative law*. _____

14. Who are known as clients? _____

15. What are SOPs? _____
    _____

16. What is the federal bureaucracy sometimes called? _____

17. What is the process of examining a department's compliance with the law and scrutinizing its budget requests? _____

18. How does Congress sometimes authorize the Government Accountability Office (GAO) to exercise checks over the bureaucracy? _____

(continued on next page)

19. What legislation provided citizens access to information previously withheld? _____

20. What is the mismanagement of money, time, and personnel by government? _____

21. List the seven major bureaucratic problems. _____

22. What is red tape? _____

23. Define *bureaucratese*. _____

24. List the four distinctive characteristics of the US bureaucracy. _____

Match the following departments with their correct definitions or descriptions.

A. Commerce
B. Defense
C. Health and Human Services
D. Homeland Security
E. Housing and Urban Development
F. Interior
G. Justice
H. Labor
I. State
J. Transportation
K. Treasury
L. Veterans Affairs

_____ 25. enforces laws regarding minimum wage and safe working conditions

_____ 26. manages national parks and public lands

_____ 27. includes the Federal Aviation Administration (FAA)

_____ 28. created after the terrorist attacks on September 11, 2001

_____ 29. collects taxes

_____ 30. advises the president regarding foreign policy; issues passports and visas

_____ 31. has the largest budget of any cabinet department

_____ 32. promotes international trade; conducts the census; issues patents and trademarks

_____ 33. headed by the Attorney General

AMERICAN GOVERNMENT

Name _____

CHAPTER 13 • ACTIVITY 1

US Foreign Policy Goals

Give an example of how the United States is currently trying to achieve each of the foreign policy goals listed in the following table.

Foreign policy goal	Example
National Security	
Alliance Security	
International Stability	
Economic Development	

AMERICAN GOVERNMENT

Name _____

CHAPTER 13 • ACTIVITY 2

Foreign Policy Development

For each of the time periods shown below, compile a list of events mentioned in the Student Edition that are associated with the four major goals of US foreign policy (national security, alliance security, international stability, or economic development). After each event, identify in parentheses which of the four goals was connected with that incident.

Time period	Events and goals
1790–1890	
1890–1910	
1910–40	

(continued on next page)

Time period	Events and goals
1941–91	
1991–present	

AMERICAN GOVERNMENT

CHAPTER 13 • ACTIVITY 3

Two Views of American Involvement in Foreign Affairs

Below are excerpts from two articles which present very different views regarding American foreign policy. Read each excerpt and answer the questions.

"Global Interventionism and the Erosion of Domestic Liberty"

There is a tendency of many people to separate domestic and foreign issues. For instance, many supporters of the free market advocate government activism abroad. But categorizing issues as "foreign policy" or "domestic policy" can be artificial and misleading. Developments in one arena frequently interact with and affect developments in the other.

The foreign policy of the United States has obviously changed dramatically since "isolationism" held sway at the end of the 1930s. . . . [Since that time] the republic has acquired and maintained a host of global political and military commitments. Washington has linked America's security to that of the other hemispheric nations through [numerous treaties and multilateral pacts]. . . . Such formal arrangements, however, do not fully measure the extent of US obligations in the world. [Many of them pledge the United States to assist nations but attach] no discernible geographic limits to that promise of assistance, and [serve] as the explicit or tacit basis for US involvement in numerous . . . struggles throughout the [world]. Moreover, growing US involvement in peacekeeping operations authorized by the U.N. Security Council . . . and "out of area" operations conducted by NATO . . . is likely to increase the total. . . .

This policy has had a pervasive impact on the Republic's domestic affairs. In ways both obvious and subtle it has transformed the nation economically, socially, and politically. . . .

Even when the nation terminated its war mobilizations, a sizable residue of enhanced governmental power always remained. Manifestations of that "wartime" authority would later surface during peacetime—often in unexpected ways. . . .

. . . America has been essentially on a war footing [since World War II] . . . and the result has been a significant erosion of liberty. . . . There are numerous examples of undesirable changes in America's domestic system brought about by Washington's global interventionist foreign policy. Waging the Cold War led to the creation of a large and expensive military establishment. . . .

. . . An interventionist foreign policy has not only facilitated the expansion of federal governmental power at the expense of the private sector, but has also produced ominous changes within the federal government itself. The conduct of foreign affairs during the Cold War enhanced the power of the executive branch to an unhealthy degree. . . .

1. Why is it difficult to separate "foreign policy" from "domestic policy"? _____
   _____

2. List ways in which US foreign policy has changed since the late 1930s. _____
   _____
   _____
   _____

3. The author says that there are "numerous examples of undesirable changes in America's domestic system" because of the nation's "global interventionist foreign policy." What are these? _____
   _____
   _____

(continued on next page)

Maintaining a global interventionist policy has led inexorably to the emergence of an "imperial presidency." Chief executives have grown accustomed to using the military according to their personal definitions of the national interest, frequently without even the semblance of congressional consent. The congressional war power, stated in clear and concise terms in the Constitution, has become [virtually non-existent]. . . .

Perhaps the most corrosive domestic effect of Washington's interventionist foreign policy has been on national attitudes. Americans have come to accept governmental intrusions in the name of "national security" that they would have ferociously opposed as blatant power grabs in earlier eras. Politicians gradually learned that the fastest way to overcome opposition to schemes to expand the state was to portray initiatives as necessary for the security of the nation. Sometimes such reasoning has been exceedingly strained. . . .

Excerpted from Ted Galen Carpenter, "Global Interventionism and the Erosion of Domestic Liberty," *The Freeman* (November 1997). Irvington-on-Hudson, NY: The Foundation for Economic Education, 1997 (www.FEE.org). Used by permission.

4. According to the author, how has American foreign policy affected the president and the Congress?

5. According to the author, how has American foreign policy affected national attitudes? _____

"The Danger of US Isolation"

For the past century, the United States has been the dominant player in global affairs and it has used its dominant position to enforce . . . political and economic order on much of the world. After its entry in the First World War turned the tide against the . . . [Central Powers], the United States emerged as the world's economic powerhouse. In the Second World War, the United States, together with its Soviet, British and other allies, ended the imperial ambitions of Germany and Japan, allowing . . . capitalist order to dominate much of Europe and Asia. Finally, the US "victory" in the Cold War resulted in much of the rest of the world being integrated into a US-led economic, trade and investment system that brought unprecedented growth to many formerly isolated areas of the world. While the United States has made many mistakes in its position of global leadership, its role as the primary enforcer of peace in Europe and Asia, and its protection of the world's leading trade routes, resulted in decades of remarkable growth in terms of economic output [for the nation]. . . .

6. Summarize what is stated in the first paragraph above. _____

(continued on next page)

7. What does the article say accounts for the remarkable growth of economic output for America?

_____

_____

Prior to its ascendancy to the top of the global power table during the Second World War, much of the United States' history was dominated by a desire to remain isolated from the problems of the rest of the world. While defending its role as the dominant power in the Western Hemisphere for the past 200 years, the United States had largely remained aloof from problems further afield and even when it was dragged into far-away conflicts, as during the First World War, it quickly retreated back into isolationism. For many, this isolationism allowed the United States to concentrate on the development, modernization and expansion of the US economy, something that resulted in the United States becoming the world's dominant economy many decades before it became the world's leading political and military power. This nostalgia for a bygone era when the United States was effectively shielded by two vast oceans from the rest of the world's problems is a key component of the renewed desire by many US voters to have the country return to a sort of 21st century isolationism. . . .

8. Prior to World War II, what dominant desire had been present in US history? _____

_____

9. What renewed desire have many US voters recently displayed? _____

_____

Polls taken in recent years have shown that there is a clear trend towards more support for a lesser role for the United States in global affairs among US voters. The endless wars in the Middle East and Central Asia, coupled with what many people in the United States see as the negative impact of the US trade and investment partnerships with foreign countries, have led to greater support for . . . the United States to focus on internal affairs, rather than on issues and threats overseas. . . . The United States' extensive military commitments in all regions of the world are also being questioned, as more and more areas of the world grow increasingly unstable. Altogether, political, security and economic trends are combining to convince many US voters that their country should turn inward, regardless of the implications.

10. What are two factors that have led many Americans to call for the United States to focus on internal

matters rather than foreign ones? _____

_____

_____

11. How do many Americans feel about the extensive military commitments around the world? _____

_____

(continued on next page)

Unfortunately for the United States and the rest of the world, the US remains the indispensable country when it comes to maintaining . . . trade and investment order that dominates the world economy, as well as the military alliances that have preserved peace in Europe and Asia in recent decades. . . . On the political and security front, a collapse of US-led defense alliances in Europe and Asia would encourage revisionist powers such as Russia and China to use force to defend their territorial claims in the former Soviet Union (for Russia) and in the waters of the western Pacific Ocean (for China). Moreover, no single power would be in a position to take the United States' place as the power guaranteeing trade, investment and security in the key economic centers of the world, leading to significantly higher levels of conflict risk around the world. As such, a turn towards isolationism in the United States would worsen, rather than enhance, the prospects for security and economic growth in the US and around the world, making the US and the world a much more dangerous place.

"The Danger of US Isolationism," *International Strategic Analysis*. (22 September 2016). (www.isa-world.com).

12. Explain what the article states would happen if the US abandoned its defense alliances in Europe and Asia.

13. Look back at the first of the two articles in this activity. Write a two-sentence summary of the information presented.

14. Write a two-sentence summary of the second article.

15. These articles present two different views of American foreign policy. Which approach to foreign policy do you think is the best? Explain your answer.

AMERICAN GOVERNMENT

Name _____

CHAPTER 13 • ACTIVITY 4

Chapter Review

Match the following terms with their correct definitions or descriptions.

A. alliance
B. consulates
C. containment
D. embassies
E. executive agreements
F. globalization
G. isolationism
H. national security
I. passport
J. rogue nation
K. sanctions
L. treaties
M. visa

_____ 1. identifies a traveler and confirms his citizenship

_____ 2. disregards international law and violates human rights

_____ 3. usually located in a foreign nation's capital

_____ 4. agreements the United States makes that require Senate approval

_____ 5. protecting the country and its citizens and property abroad

_____ 6. measures taken against a nation to influence its actions

_____ 7. agreements made with foreign nations that do not require congressional approval

_____ 8. an arrangement that unites its participants in a common cause

_____ 9. strategy the US used in dealing with communism during the Cold War

_____ 10. belief that America should not be tied to another nation

Match the following terms with their correct definitions or descriptions.

A. Economic and Social Council
B. General Assembly
C. Human Rights Council
D. International Court of Justice
E. Secretariat
F. Security Council
G. Trusteeship Council

_____ 11. located in the The Hague, Netherlands

_____ 12. consists of fifteen members

_____ 13. no longer in operation

_____ 14. consists of one voting delegate from each member country

_____ 15. main administrative body of the UN

(continued on next page)

Answer the following questions.

16. What are the four goals of US foreign policy? _____

17. Explain the strategy of mutual assured destruction (MAD)? _____

18. Which terrorist group was responsible for the attacks on September 11, 2001? _____

19. What is the title for the official who acts as the president's personal representative to a foreign country? _____

20. What is the name for the Defense Department headquarters in Arlington, Virginia? _____

21. What group consists of the nation's top military officers? _____

22. What new department was created after the September 11, 2001, terrorist attacks? _____

23. What is globalization? _____

24. List four well-known Muslim extremist groups. _____

Match the following terms with their correct definitions or descriptions.

A. European Union (EU)
B. League of Nations
C. Marshall Plan
D. Monroe Doctrine
E. National Security Council (NSC)
F. North American Free Trade Agreement (NAFTA)
G. North Atlantic Treaty Organization (NATO)
H. United Nations (UN)
I. US Agency for International Development (USAID)
J. World Trade Organization (WTO)

_____ 25. delivers money, food, and health and education services to assist foreign countries

_____ 26. stated opposition to any European presence in the Western Hemisphere

_____ 27. created at the end of World War II (1945)

_____ 28. replaced the General Agreement on Tariffs and Trade (GATT)

_____ 29. provides information and guidance for the president on matters regarding the safety of Americans

_____ 30. eliminated tariffs and introduced a common currency

_____ 31. involved only three nations

_____ 32. gave billions of dollars to western Europe to rebuild after World War II

_____ 33. participants agree to assist each other in case of attack

AMERICAN GOVERNMENT

Name _____

CHAPTER 14 • ACTIVITY 1

The Principles of Blackstone's *Commentaries*

Below are excerpts from an article dealing with the foundational principles described in Sir William Blackstone's *Commentaries on the Laws of England*. The quoted portions are directly from that work. Read the selection and answer the questions that follow.

Several foundational principles are expressed in both the Judeo-Christian worldview and Blackstone's *Commentaries*. These principles [are] summarized below. . . .

There are different types of law in the universe. Blackstone's classification of law into six types is foundational to the rest of his philosophy and is consistent with the Judeo-Christian system of law:

Law as the order of the universe. "Thus when the Supreme Being formed the universe, and created matter out of nothing, He impressed certain principles upon that matter, from which it can never depart, and without which it would cease to be."

Law as a rule of human action. ". . . The precepts by which man, the noblest of all sublunary [earthly] beings, a creature endowed with both reason and free will, is commanded to make use of those faculties in the general regulation of his behavior."

Law of nature. "These are the eternal, immutable [enduring] laws of good and evil, to which the Creator Himself in all His dispensations conforms; and which He has enabled human reason to discover, so far as they are necessary for the conduct of human actions."

Revealed law. "The doctrines . . . delivered [by an immediate and direct revelation] we call the revealed or divine law, and they are to be found only in the Holy Scriptures. . . . Upon these two foundations, the law of nature and the law of revelation, depend all human laws; that is to say, no human laws should be suffered to contradict these."

Law of nations. "As it is impossible for the whole race of mankind to be united in one great society, they must necessarily divide into many. . . . [The regulation of their interaction]. . . depends entirely upon the rules of natural law, or upon mutual compacts, treaties, leagues, and agreements. . . ."

Municipal law. "[This is] a rule of civil conduct, prescribed by the supreme power in a state, commanding what is right and prohibiting what is wrong. But no human authority can act without limits."

1. List the six types of laws that Blackstone discussed in his writings. _____
   _____
   _____

2. Blackstone identifies two traits with which all humans are endowed. What are those, and how does he say those should be used? _____
   _____

3. On what two laws does Blackstone say all human laws depend? _____
   _____

(continued on next page)

The author lists a number of principles that are prevalent in Blackstone's writings. Read the list and answer the questions that follow.

God is not only the Creator, but a Being of infinite power, wisdom, and goodness.

God created man and His fundamental laws in such a way that man can be happy only when he is obeying God's law. . . .

The purpose of human law is to "command what is right, prohibiting what is wrong."

Human law is not to violate God's law. . . .

Human law's most effectual tool for producing right conduct and preventing wrong conduct is sanctions—punishment. . . .

There are three primary personal rights:

Personal security. The right . . . consists in a person's legal and uninterrupted enjoyment of his life, his limbs, his body, his health, and his reputation.

Personal liberty. This personal liberty consists in the power of locomotion [movement], of changing situation, or removing one's person to whatsoever place one's own inclination may direct; without imprisonment or restraint, unless by due course of law.

Right of private property: law of the land. [This right] consists in the free use, enjoyment, and disposal [by man] of all his acquisitions. . . .

Human judges are empowered to interpret the will of the legislature by certain distinct standards, including:

The usual meaning of words;

Context of the words being interpreted;

Subject matter of the law;

Effect of the interpretation—absurd meanings must be avoided;

The reason for the law—why it was promulgated [established].

"The Principles of Blackstone's Commentaries" from excerpts found at www.blackstoneinstitute.org/sirwilliamblackstone.html by Dr. Virgina Armstrong. Copyright © 2004-2012 Blackstone Institute. The Blackstone Institute has become a unique pioneer in creating and teaching studies in the newly-recognized field of 'constitutional/legal apologetics'."

4. According to Blackstone, what are the three primary personal rights? _____

5. What freedom is an important part of personal liberty? _____

6. What standards are human judges to use in interpreting the will of the legislature? _____

7. Identify some ways in which Blackstone's principles, outlined in this selection, are not followed by the American legal system. _____

AMERICAN GOVERNMENT

Name _____

CHAPTER 14 • ACTIVITY 3

Marbury v. Madison (1803)

Read the following summary of the famous *Marbury v. Madison* Supreme Court decision and the reasoning behind the Court's ruling. Then answer the questions that follow.

Facts—In compliance with the Judiciary Act of 1801, President John Adams signed a commission for William Marbury as a justice of the peace for the county of Washington, D.C. The seal of the United States was affixed to the commission, but it never reached Marbury. James Madison, the incoming secretary of state under Jefferson (a Democratic-Republican rather than a Federalist) refused to deliver the commission. Marbury went directly to the US Supreme Court for a writ of mandamus [Latin for "we command"] requiring Secretary of State Madison to deliver to Marbury his commission. The Judiciary Act of 1789 in Section 13 had provided that the Supreme Court could issue writs of mandamus.

Questions [facing the Supreme Court]—(a) Has the applicant a right to the commission he demands? (b) If that right has been violated, do the laws of the United States afford him a remedy? (c) Is this remedy a mandamus issuing from the Supreme Court? (d) The question that Marshall does not state, but for which this decision is most famous, is can the Supreme Court void an act of national legislation that it considers to be unconstitutional?

Decisions [made by the Supreme Court]—(a) Yes; (b) Yes; (c) No; (d) Yes.

Reasons—*C.J. Marshall* (5–0). By signing Marbury's commission, President Adams appointed him a justice of the peace. The seal of the United States affixed thereto by the secretary of state was conclusive testimony of the legitimacy of the signature, and of the completion of the appointment. That appointment, under its terms, conferred on Marbury a legal right to the office for the space of five years. Thus, Marbury had a right to the commission he demanded.

Where there is a legal right, there is also a legal remedy by suit, or action at law, whenever that right is invaded. Marbury had a legal right, and this right was obviously violated by Madison's refusal to deliver to him the commission. Thus a remedy under United States laws was due Marbury.

1. To what position was William Marbury commissioned by President Adams? _____

2. Why was Adams's commissioning of Marbury never official? _____

3. What was Marbury asking the Supreme Court to do? _____

4. According to the Supreme Court, was Marbury entitled to the commission he sought? _____

The Supreme Court of the United States had no power to issue a mandamus to the secretary of state since this would be an exercise of original jurisdiction not warranted by the Constitution. Congress had no power to enlarge the Supreme Court's original jurisdiction beyond the limited circumstances involving diplomatic personnel [ambassadors, other public ministers, and consuls] and disputes among the states described in Article III of the Constitution.

(continued on next page)

5. Explain why the Supreme Court did not demand that Madison deliver the commission to Marbury. _Sentence Morin privilage government and indipendent_

The people designed the Constitution as a written instrument designed to control government. The Constitution is "either a superior paramount law, unchangeable by ordinary means, or it is on a level with ordinary legislative acts [like the provision of the Judiciary Act in question]." Marshall argued that the Constitution was in the former category of fundamental law and that "it is emphatically the province and duty of the judicial department to say what the law is."

6. Why was the Constitution designed? _____

7. In your own words, explain two competing views of the Constitution. _____

8. What two things did Chief Justice John Marshall argue? _____

When faced with a conflict between an unconstitutional law (as further examples, Marshall cited cases where a state lays a prohibited export tax, adopts a bill of attainder or ex post facto law, or flouts constitutional guidelines regarding convictions for treason) and the Constitution, the judges, who take an oath to uphold the Constitution, must enforce the more fundamental law. Otherwise, provisions of the Constitution could be flouted with impunity. Judges take an oath to uphold the US Constitution: "Why does a judge swear to discharge his duties agreeably to the constitution of the United States, if that constitution forms no rule for his government? if it is closed upon him, and cannot be inspected by him?" Marshall also noted that the supremacy clause in Article VI of the Constitution makes "the constitution itself" the supreme law of the land.

Note—This is the first time the Court declared an act of Congress unconstitutional, and thus established the doctrine of judicial review. It was not until a half century later in *Dred Scott v. Sandford*, 19 Howard 393 (1857) that the Court was to do it again.

John R. Vile, *Essential Supreme Court Decisions*, 15th ed. (New York: Rowman and Littlefield, 2010), 105–6.

9. What does John Marshall say must be done if there is a conflict between an unconstitutional law and the Constitution? _____

10. What did the Supreme Court do, for the first time, by rendering its decision in *Marbury v. Madison*? _____

11. What doctrine did this case establish? _____

12. When and in what decision did the Supreme Court next exercise the sort of power that it applied in this case? _____

AMERICAN GOVERNMENT

Name _____

CHAPTER 14 • ACTIVITY 4

The Originalist Perspective

Read the following explanation of "originalism" by David F. Forte of The Heritage Foundation. Then answer the questions that follow.

Written constitutionalism implies that those who make, interpret, and enforce the law ought to be guided by the meaning of the United States Constitution—the supreme law of the land—as it was originally written. This view came to be seriously eroded over the course of the last century with the rise of the theory of the Constitution as a "living document" with no fixed meaning, subject to changing interpretations according to the spirit of the times. . . .

Originalism is championed for a number of fundamental reasons. First, it comports [conforms, harmonizes] with the nature of a constitution, which binds and limits any one generation from ruling according to the passion of the times. The Framers of the Constitution of 1787 knew what they were about, forming a frame of government for "ourselves and our Posterity." They did not understand "We the people" to be merely an assemblage of individuals at any one point in time but a "people" as an association, indeed a number of overlapping associations, over the course of many generations, including our own. In the end, the Constitution of 1787 is as much a constitution for us as it was for the Founding generation.

Second, originalism supports legitimate popular government that is accountable. The Framers believed that a form of government accountable to the people, leaving them fundamentally in charge of their own destinies, best protected human liberty. . . .

1. What view of the Constitution has led to the erosion of the view that the Constitution should be interpreted as it was originally written? _____

_____

2. How does the clause "for ourselves and our Posterity" relate to the debate over the meaning of the Constitution? _____

_____

Third, originalism accords with [agrees with] the constitutional purpose of limiting government. It understands the several parts of the federal government to be creatures [creations] of the Constitution, and to have no legitimate existence outside of the Constitution. The authority of these various entities extends no further than what was devolved [delegated] upon them by the Constitution. . . .

Fourth, it follows that originalism limits the judiciary. It prevents the Supreme Court from asserting its will over the careful mix of institutional arrangements that are charged with making policy, each accountable in various ways to the people. . . .

Fifth, . . . originalism comports [conforms, harmonizes] with the understanding of what our Constitution was to be by the people who formed and ratified that document. It affirms that the Constitution is a coherent and interrelated document, with subtle balances incorporated throughout. Reflecting the Founders' understanding of the self-motivated impulses of human nature, the Constitution erected devices that work to frustrate those impulses. . . .

3. How does originalism accord with the principle of limited government? _____

_____

_____

(continued on next page)

4. What did the Founders understand about human nature? _____

   Sixth, originalism, properly pursued, is not result-oriented, whereas much nonoriginalist writing is patently so. If evidence demonstrates that the Framers understood the commerce power, for example, to be broader than we might wish, then the originalist ethically must accept the conclusion. . . . The concept of the Constitution of 1787 as a good first draft in need of constant revision and updating—encapsulated in vague phrases such as the "living Constitution"—merely turns the Constitution into an unwritten charter to be developed by the contemporary values of sitting judges. . . .

5. What concept does the author warn against? In your own words, what does the author say that following that concept will produce? _____

   How does one go about ascertaining the original meaning of the Constitution? All originalists begin with the text of the Constitution, the words of a particular clause. In the search for the meaning of the text and its legal effect, originalist researchers variously look to the following:
   The evident meaning of the words.
   The meaning according to the lexicon of the times.
   The meaning in context with other sections of the Constitution.
   The meaning according to the words by the Framer suggesting the language.
   The elucidation [clarification] of the meaning by debate within the Constitutional Convention.
   The historical provenance [background] of the words, particularly their legal history.
   The words in the context of the contemporaneous social, economic, and political events.
   The words in the context of the revolutionary struggle.
   The words in the context of the political philosophy shared by the Founding generation. . . .
   Historical, religious, and philosophical authority put forward by the Framers.
   The commentary in the ratification debates.
   The commentary by contemporaneous interpreters, such as Publius in *The Federalist*.
   The subsequent historical practice by the Founding generation to exemplify the understood meaning. . . .
   Early judicial interpretations.
   Evidence of long-standing traditions that demonstrate the people's understanding of the words. . . .
   Originalism does not remove controversy, or disagreement, but it does cabin it within a principled constitutional tradition that makes real the Rule of Law. Without that, we are destined, as Aristotle warned long ago, to fall into the "rule of men."

   David F. Forte, "The Originalist Perspective," in *The Heritage Guide to the Constitution* (Washington, DC: The Heritage Foundation, 2005). Used by permission.

6. Write a brief paragraph explaining how originalists determine the meaning of the various clauses of the Constitution. _____

7. What do you think are some reasons a person might oppose interpreting the Constitution from an originalist perspective? _____

AMERICAN GOVERNMENT

Name _____

CHAPTER 15 • ACTIVITY 2

First Amendment Freedoms

Issues involving each of our five First Amendment freedoms continue to arise. Give a recent example where each freedom has been a matter of controversy. Explain whether you think that freedom was protected in the instance you cite.

Freedom of Religion

_____
_____
_____
_____

Freedom of Speech

_____
_____
_____
_____

Freedom of the Press

_____
_____
_____
_____

Freedom of Assembly

_____
_____
_____
_____

Freedom of Petition

_____
_____
_____
_____

AMERICAN GOVERNMENT

Name _____

CHAPTER 15 • ACTIVITY 3

The Second Amendment

Read the Second Amendment below and answer the questions that follow. You may need to refer to outside sources.

A well regulated militia, being necessary to the security of a free state, the right of the people to keep and bear arms, shall not be infringed.

1. What do the first thirteen words of the twenty-seven word amendment say? _____

2. What was a militia at the time the amendment was adopted in 1791? _____

3. What are "arms"? _____

4. Americans argue about the amendment's meaning. Some interpret it as protection of **collective rights**, and others say it protects **individual rights**. What do you think is the difference between these views?

5. Why do you think there has been so much debate in your lifetime about the "right to bear arms"?

6. Do you think there should be limitations (background checks before purchase, limit on types or number of weapons, etc.) on guns? Explain your answer. _____

AMERICAN GOVERNMENT

Name _____

CHAPTER 15 • ACTIVITY 4

The Duties of Citizenship

Read the following radio address, delivered by President Calvin Coolidge from the White House on November 3, 1924. Then answer the questions that follow.

The people of our country are sovereign. They have no right to say they do not care. They must care!

The institutions of our country rest upon faith in the people. . . . Each one of us who is qualified [should] vote. That is a function which cannot be delegated, which cannot be postponed. The opportunity will never arise again. If the individual fails to discharge that obligation, the whole nation will suffer a loss from that neglect.

America, more thoroughly than any other country, has adopted a system of self-government. Sometimes we refer to it as the rule of the people. Certainly it is a system under which there is every opportunity for self-government and every encouragement for the people to rule. Ours has been described as a government of public opinion. Of course, public opinion functions all the time. It no doubt has its influence on the actions of the executive and legislative branches of our Government, and even though it be imperceptible [unnoticeable] on any given occasion it is probably, as time passes, reflected in the courts. But all the influence of public opinion, all the opportunity for self-government through the rule of the people, depends upon one single factor. That is the ballot box. If the time comes when our citizens fail to respond to their right and duty, individually and collectively, intelligently and effectively at the ballot box on election day, I do not know what form of government will be substituted for that which we at present have the opportunity to enjoy, but I do know it will no longer be a rule of the people, it will no longer be self-government. The people of our country are sovereign. If they do not vote they abdicate that sovereignty, and they may be entirely sure that if they relinquish it other forces will seize it, and if they fail to govern themselves some other power will rise up to govern them. The choice is always before them, whether they will be slaves or whether they will be free. The only way to be free is to exercise actively and energetically the privileges, and discharge faithfully the duties which make freedom. It is not to be secured by passive resistance. It is the result of energy and action.

1. Within the context of this radio address, what did Coolidge consider the highest duty of an American citizen? _____

2. Who suffers if individuals do not vote? _____

3. What does Coolidge say will happen if people fail to cast ballots on election day? _____

4. What will happen if people fail to govern themselves? _____

5. What choice always faces Americans? _____

6. What is the only way Americans can be free? _____

(continued on next page)

To live up to the full measure of citizenship in this nation requires not only action, but it requires intelligent action. It is necessary to secure information and to acquire education. The background of our citizenship is the meeting house and the school house, the place of religious worship and the place of intellectual training. But we cannot abandon our education at the school house door. We have to keep it up through life. A political campaign can be justified only on the grounds that it enables the citizens to become informed as to what policies are best for themselves and for their country, in order that they may vote to elect those who from their past record and present professions they know will put such policies into effect. The purpose of a campaign is to send an intelligent and informed voter to the ballot box. . . .

We are always confronted with the question of whether we wish to be ruled by all the people or a part of the people, by the minority or the majority; whether we wish our elections to be dominated by those who have been misled, through the presentation of half-truths, into the formation of hasty, illogical and unsound conclusions; or whether we wish those to determine the course of our Government who have through due deliberation and careful consideration of all the factors involved reached a sound and mature conclusion. We shall always have with us an element of discontent, an element inspired with more zeal than knowledge. They will always be active and energetic, and they seldom fail to vote on election day. But the people at large in this country are not represented by them. They are greatly in the minority. But their number is large enough to be a decisive factor in many elections, unless it is offset by the sober second thought of the people who have something at stake, whether it be earnings from investment or from employment, who are considering not only their own welfare, but the welfare of their children and of coming generations. . . .

But the right to vote is conferred upon our citizens not only that they may exercise it for their own benefit but also for the benefit of others. Persons who have the right to vote are trustees for the benefit of their country and their countrymen. They have no right to say they do not care. They must care! They have no right to say that whatever the result of the election they can get along. They must remember that their country and their countrymen cannot get along, cannot remain sound, cannot preserve its institutions, cannot protect its citizens, cannot maintain its place in the world, unless those who have the right to vote do sustain and do guide the course of public affairs by the thoughtful exercise of that right on election day. They do not hold a mere privilege to be exercised or not, as passing fancy may move them. They are charged with a great trust, one of the most important and most solemn which can be given into the keeping of an American citizen. It should be discharged thoughtfully and seriously, in accordance with its vast importance.

7. What is the purpose of a political campaign? _____

8. What are two reasons the right to vote is conferred on people? _____

9. According to Coolidge, what five things cannot be done if people do not vote? _____

10. Statistics show that the percentage of young voters (ages 18 to 24) in any election is typically low. Why do you think that is the case? What can be done to increase that percentage? _____

AMERICAN GOVERNMENT

Name _____

CHAPTER 16 • ACTIVITY 1

Party Functions

US political parties have four important functions: (1) nominating candidates, (2) governing, (3) acting as watchdogs of the opposition, and (4) providing a moderating influence. Choose one of the two major US parties and, using various media sources, give an example of how that party illustrates each function. Include the media source(s) used for each example.

Political Party _____

Candidate Nomination
Cite three recent candidates from this party (local, state, or national level).

_____
_____
_____

Governing
How many members does the party have in the US House of Representatives? The US Senate? Is your state's governor from this party?

_____
_____

Watchdog
List recent actions members of this party have taken to show concern about or opposition to something done by another political party.

_____
_____
_____
_____
_____

Moderating Influence
Cite compromises within the party concerning legislation or about a particular issue.

_____
_____
_____
_____
_____

AMERICAN GOVERNMENT

Name _____

CHAPTER 16 • ACTIVITY 2

Voter Turnout in Presidential Elections

Study the following line graph showing voter turnout since 1828. Then answer the questions.

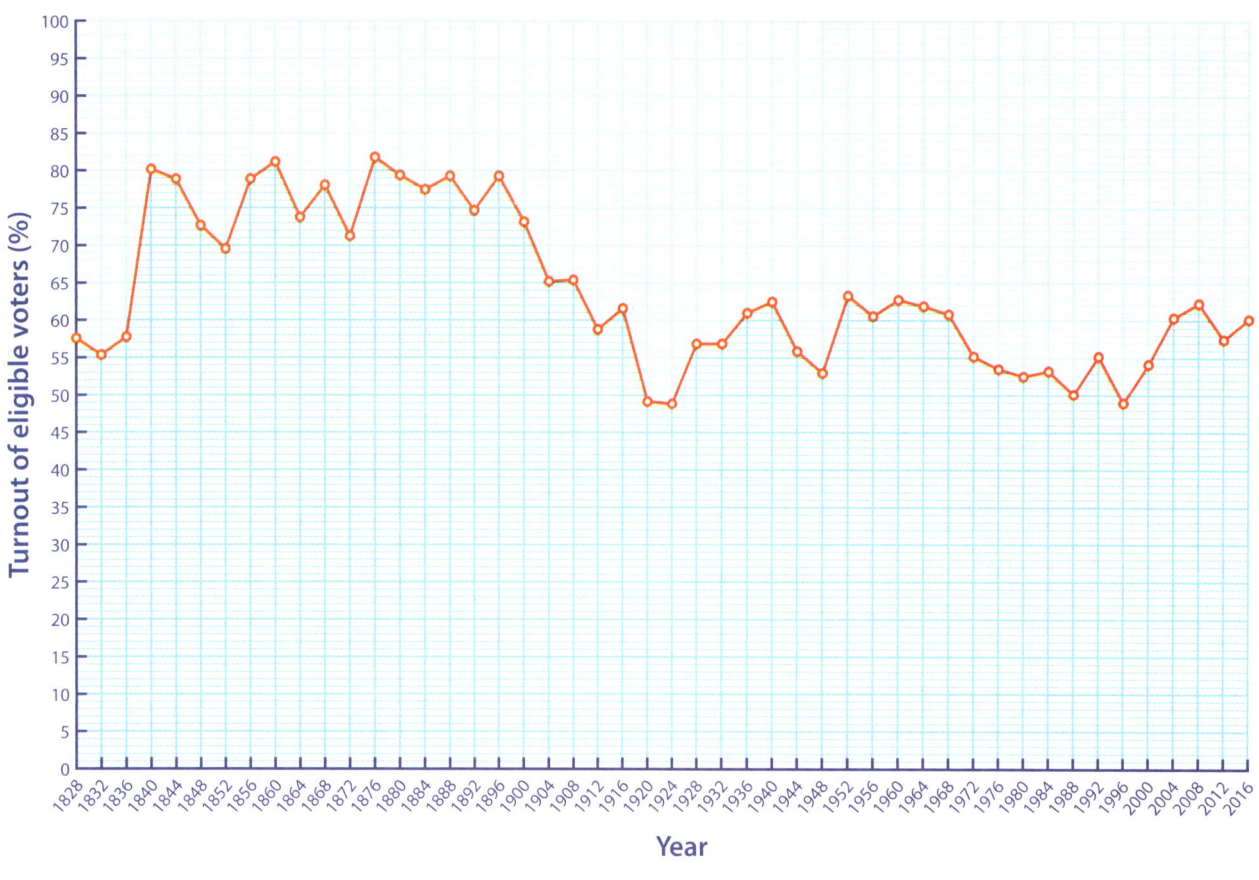

1. In which three elections was voter turnout the lowest? _____

2. In which three elections was voter turnout the highest? _____

3. What factors influence voter turnout? _____

_____

_____

_____

4. Is low voter turnout a bad thing? Should greater efforts be exerted to get more people to vote? If so, how could that be accomplished? _____

_____

_____

_____

AMERICAN GOVERNMENT

Name _____

CHAPTER 16 • ACTIVITY 3

Washington's Farewell Address

On September 19, 1796, after serving two presidential terms, President Washington had his farewell address published in Philadelphia's *American Daily Advertiser*. One matter he emphasized was the dangers of political parties. Read each excerpt and answer the questions.

"In contemplating the causes which may disturb our Union, it occurs as matter of serious concern that any ground should have been furnished for characterizing [political] parties by geographical discriminations [locations], Northern and Southern, Atlantic and Western; whence, designing men may endeavor to excite a belief that there is a real difference of local interests and views."

1. Give one reason for the formation of political parties _____

"All obstructions to the execution of the laws, all combinations and associations, under whatever plausible character, with the real design to direct, control, counteract, or awe the regular deliberation and action of the constituted authorities, are destructive of this fundamental principle, and of fatal tendency. They serve to organize faction, to give it an artificial and extraordinary force; to put, in the place of the delegated will of the nation the will of a party, often a small but artful and enterprising minority of the community. . . .

"However combinations or associations of the above description may now and then answer popular ends, they are likely, in the course of time and things, to become potent engines, by which cunning, ambitious, and unprincipled men will be enabled to subvert the power of the people and to usurp [take] for themselves the reins of government."

2. What is destructive to the execution of the laws? _____

3. What could take the place of the will of the nation? _____

4. What does Washington say that these "combinations or associations" (political parties) are likely to become? _____

(continued on next page)

"I have already intimated to you the danger of [political] parties in the State, with particular reference to the founding of them on geographical discriminations. Let me now take a more comprehensive view, and warn you in the most solemn manner against the baneful [destructive] effects of the spirit of party generally.

"This spirit, unfortunately, is inseparable from our nature, having its root in the strongest passions of the human mind. It exists under different shapes in all governments . . . and is truly their worst enemy.

"The alternate domination of one faction over another, sharpened by the spirit of revenge, natural to party dissension, which in different ages and countries has perpetrated the most horrid enormities [evils] is itself a frightful despotism. . . . The disorders and miseries which result gradually incline the minds of men to seek security and repose [relief, peace] in the absolute power of an individual; and sooner or later the chief of some prevailing faction, more able or more fortunate than his competitors, turns this disposition to the purposes of his own elevation, on the ruins of public liberty."

5. How is the "spirit" of the [political] party described? _____

6. What often results from feuding political parties? _____

"There is an opinion that parties in free countries are useful checks upon the administration of the government and serve to keep alive the spirit of liberty. This within certain limits is probably true; and in governments of a monarchical cast, patriotism may look with indulgence [acceptance], if not with favor, upon the spirit of party. But in those of the popular character [a democratic government], in governments purely elective, it is a spirit not to be encouraged. . . . And there being constant danger of excess, the effort ought to be by force of public opinion, to mitigate [weaken] and assuage [reduce] it."

7. How do free countries tend to look at political parties? _____

8. Political parties should not be encouraged because they pose what danger? What do you think this means? _____

9. What effect should public opinion have on the spirit of political parties? _____

Class Discussion: Was Washington correct in his assumptions about political parties? Support your answer.

AMERICAN GOVERNMENT

Name _____

CHAPTER 16 • ACTIVITY 4

Third Parties in American Politics

Select one of the following third parties and, using outside resources, research it to answer the questions.

Communist Party USA	Libertarian Party	Reform Party
Constitution Party	Progressive Party	Socialist Party USA
Green Party	Prohibition Party	Socialist Workers Party

Party Chosen: _____

1. When was the party formed? What condition or situation prompted its founding? _____
   _____

2. Who was the party's first presidential candidate? _____

3. Who was the party's most recent presidential candidate? _____

4. Summarize the party's traditional beliefs. (What does the party support and oppose?) _____
   _____
   _____
   _____
   _____

5. In your opinion, with which of the two major parties is this party in closest agreement?
   _____

6. What, if any, influence has the party had on the policies of either of the two major parties?
   _____
   _____

7. What do you think are the prospects for this party in future elections? _____
   _____
   _____

8. Do you think third parties generally have a positive, a negative, or a neutral effect on American politics? Why? _____
   _____
   _____
   _____

AMERICAN GOVERNMENT

CHAPTER 16 • ACTIVITY 5

Chapter Review

Define each term.

1. political party _____
2. nominate _____
3. partisanship _____
4. Solid South _____
   _____
5. single-member districts _____
6. bipartisan _____
7. party platform _____
8. liberal _____
   _____
9. conservative _____
   _____
10. coalition _____
11. convention _____
    _____
12. delegates _____
13. caucus _____
14. patronage _____
15. primary _____
    _____
    _____
16. Republican National Committee _____
    _____
    _____
    _____

(continued on next page)

17. Democratic National Committee _____
_____
_____

18. wards _____

19. precincts _____

20. presidential primary _____
_____

21. interest groups _____

22. independents, or independent voters _____

23. ticket splitting _____

Match the following terms with their descriptions.

A. Anti-Federalists
B. Democrats
C. Federalists
D. Green Party
E. Libertarians
F. Progressive Party
G. Republicans
H. Whigs

_____ 24. controlled the presidency for almost the entire period from 1860 to 1932

_____ 25. conservative on economic matters and liberal on social issues

_____ 26. won the popular vote in the 2016 election

_____ 27. supported ratification of the Constitution

_____ 28. nominated William Henry Harrison for the presidency

Match each person with his description.

A. John Quincy Adams
B. Henry Clay
C. Grover Cleveland
D. Alexander Hamilton
E. William Henry Harrison
F. Abraham Lincoln
G. Andrew Jackson
H. Thomas Jefferson

_____ 29. "Tippecanoe and Tyler too!"

_____ 30. accused his opponent of making a "corrupt bargain"

_____ 31. earliest leader of the Democratic-Republicans

_____ 32. leader of the Federalist Party

_____ 33. won the election of 1824

AMERICAN GOVERNMENT

Name _____

CHAPTER 17 · ACTIVITY 1

Becoming a Candidate

Imagine that you want to become a candidate from your district for a seat in the state House of Representatives. Using outside resources, provide the following information.

1. List the constitutional requirements to be a candidate for the office. _____
   _____
   _____
   _____

2. List any papers/forms that must be filed and the dates by which each must be completed. _____
   _____
   _____
   _____

3. List any fee(s) that must be paid. _____
   _____
   _____
   _____

4. Write a press statement announcing your candidacy and highlighting your qualifications and positions.
   _____
   _____
   _____
   _____
   _____
   _____
   _____
   _____

(continued on next page)

5. Write a brief autobiography to be submitted to media outlets.

6. List three issues important to your district and give your position on each issue.

   Issue 1

   Issue 2

   Issue 3

AMERICAN GOVERNMENT

CHAPTER 17 • ACTIVITY 2

The Role of New Media in Political Campaigning

The "new media"—Facebook, Instagram, Twitter, blogs, websites, text messages, etc.—have become a potent tool in conducting political campaigns. Read the following excerpts from an article by Courtney Mitchell of the *University Gazette* about the studies of Daniel Kreiss, assistant professor in the School of Journalism and Mass Communication at the University of North Carolina at Chapel Hill. Then answer the questions.

In 2000, the websites for Al Gore and George [W.] Bush were mostly print brochures with URLs. But [Howard] Dean's site [during his 2004 campaign for the Democratic nomination for president] had moving parts that gave his supporters the ability to participate with one another across geographic and demographic lines. Kreiss saw those supporters spreading Dean's message through emails and blogs and arranging get-togethers through Meetup.com. . . .

"Campaigns need money and they need boots on the ground to knock on doors; they need people driving their message for them," Kreiss said. "Dean's campaign pioneered how you harness this incredible energy that revolves around candidates to make it work for you. . . ."

Kreiss said staffers working in broadcast communications and high donor fundraising struggled to get a handle on this new portion of the electorate who could use new media to canvass and create buzz in their own circles.

With each passing election, many of these same players have stayed involved with the party, perfecting tools and creating technology in the off years [non-election years] to reach and engage more voters the next time around.

"Campaigns want to reach out to folks who are supporting them and have those people pass on their message in their social networks," Kreiss said. "There's an idea that you'll find it more credible as a voter to see information coming from one of your friends rather than a political campaign. . . ."

"Using new media has lowered the costs of . . . volunteering and engaging in these sorts of civic activities," Kreiss said. "More people can make phone calls or give small donations. It's much more efficient in where you're going to spend your resources."

1. Which candidate was responsible for advancing the "new media revolution" in political campaigning? When and under what circumstances did this occur? _____

2. How did that person's website differ from those of Al Gore and George W. Bush in 2000? _____

3. Why do some people find more credibility in political messages sent and received via new media? _____

4. What are some advantages of using new media for political campaigning? _____

(continued on next page)

New media have enhanced a campaign's capability to collect and leverage voter data, and to target voters based on what their activities say about them. . . .

Campaigns use Internet browsing history, grocery store card purchases, spending habits, real estate records and hundreds of other points of data to optimize their approach.

An unregistered voter in a swing state might get a more general email, while someone who created a profile on [a candidate's] site may be asked to donate, Kreiss said. Sites test colors and copy to see what increases the likelihood of a specific voter taking a specific action.

"In 2008, Obama's team designed over 2,000 different versions of their webpage alone," Kreiss said.

Though many may not be aware of the extent to which their data is [sic] recorded, it's nothing new, Kreiss said. In the early 1900s, William Jennings Bryan's family helped create a file on voters based on the information in their letters of support. Direct mail has long been a way to profile people and infer political preferences from that information.

It isn't behavioral theory, Kreiss said, it's formula. "At the end of the day, what they care about is increasing the probability that you're going to do x, y or z. . . ."

Kreiss is looking at a busy election season as he investigates what's different about 2012. "For one thing, a lot more people are writing in public about elections," Kreiss said. . . .

"The Internet is not only embedded in the fabric of our lives, it is fast becoming the central way that we act and express ourselves as democratic citizens," [Kreiss] said. "We all share the responsibility to make sure that we can have robust and inclusive political participation and debate."

Used by permission by the *University Gazette* at the University of North Carolina at Chapel Hill.

5. In what ways do users of new media collect data on the potential recipients of their messages?

6. How does it make you feel that political campaigns can gather so much personal information about you?

7. How do campaign workers test their media messages?

8. Which historical political figure, more than a century ago, was a forerunner of this scientific database building for political purposes? How did he do so?

9. What does Daniel Kreiss say is "embedded in the fabric of our lives"?

10. Have you received any political contacts through any forms of new media that you use? If so, describe each of them and the effect (if any) it had on your political positions or decision making.

11. Have you done any work for a political campaign using new media? If so, describe it.

AMERICAN GOVERNMENT

Name _____

CHAPTER 17 • ACTIVITY 3

State Election Laws

Using outside resources, answer the following questions concerning your state's election laws.

1. What are the voter qualifications for your state? _____
   _____

2. What are the voter registration deadlines? _____
   _____

3. What are the rules regarding absentee voting? _____
   _____
   _____

4. If early voting is available, when does it begin? _____
   _____

5. When are absentee ballots counted? _____
   _____

6. Which Election Day workers are present at the polling places? What are the minimum qualifications for poll workers? What (if anything) are they paid? _____
   _____
   _____

7. What provisions are made for making polling places accessible to the elderly and disabled?
   _____
   _____

8. When may a post-election recount be requested? What are the rules/laws regarding recounts?
   _____
   _____
   _____

9. What does it mean that election results must be certified? Explain the deadline(s) for this certification.
   _____
   _____
   _____

AMERICAN GOVERNMENT

Name _____

CHAPTER 17 • ACTIVITY 4

Summarizing Recent Elections

Using outside sources, answer the following.

1. Use the chart below to enter the results of the most recent presidential election.

Presidential Election Votes					
Party	Candidate Name	National Popular Vote	National Electoral College Vote	Your State's Popular Vote	Your State's Electoral College Vote
Democrat					
Republican					

2. If in the most recent election a third-party presidential candidate obtained more than 10 percent of the national popular vote and/or received any electoral votes, list the candidate and those results.

   _____

   _____

3. In the most recent election, who were the candidates for your US Representative seat, and what were the vote totals for each? _____

   _____

   _____

4. List the name and party affiliation of each winner for the most recent state elections.

   Office   **Winner/Party**

   _____

   _____

   _____

   _____

5. List the name and party affiliation of each winner for the most recent local (county or municipal) election.

   Office   **Winner/Party**

   _____

   _____

   _____

   _____

AMERICAN GOVERNMENT

Name _____

CHAPTER 17 • ACTIVITY 5

Chapter Review

Answer the following questions.

1. Define *nomination*. _____

2. What is an important first step toward being elected to office? _____
   _____

3. What does *incumbent* mean? _____

4. List three categories of campaign workers. _____

5. List the four methods of nominating a candidate. _____

6. What term means a formal document signed by a required number of qualified voters on behalf of a candidate in an election district? _____

7. What is a preliminary election held to select the party's candidate for general election and/or elect delegates to a political party's conventions? _____

8. Define *closed primary*. _____
   _____

9. What term means a primary in which voters do not have to declare their party membership?
   _____

10. What term is used for a primary in which every voter received a ballot listing all party candidates for nomination? _____

11. Explain the Top-Two method. _____
    _____
    _____

12. What is another name for the Top-Two method? _____

13. What is the name of the election in which winners of the primaries face each other? _____

14. When are general elections held? _____

15. What are constituents? _____

16. What term is used when a strong candidate on the ballot helps attract voters to other candidates from the same party? _____

(continued on next page)

153

17. What term means voting for all the candidates in one party? _____

18. What term means paid advertisements used by state and local candidates? _____

19. What is "free media" on television? _____
_____

20. Which form of social media is Donald Trump most known for using? _____

21. Which amendment allowed senators to be elected directly by the people? _____

22. What is the term for a location in a specific precinct where residents of that area go to vote?
_____

23. What did the Twenty-Sixth Amendment do? _____

24. Explain the National Voter Registration Act. _____
_____
_____

25. Who is the only Catholic to be elected president? _____

26. What is another name for a secret ballot? _____

27. What are voters called who are unable to vote in person during regular voting times? _____

28. What is *soft money*? _____
_____
_____
_____

29. What are PACs? _____
_____
_____

30. What term means money spent by a person or group that tries to help elect or defeat a candidate without the candidate's knowledge or support? _____

31. In which case did the US Supreme Court rule that the First Amendment was violated by restricting a candidate's spending of his own money for campaign purposes? _____

32. What is the Bipartisan Campaign Reform Act (BCRA) of 2002 often called? _____

33. In which case did the US Supreme Court rule that it was unconstitutional to bar corporations and unions from spending money to support or denounce individuals in elections? _____
_____

AMERICAN GOVERNMENT

Name _____

CHAPTER 18 • ACTIVITY 1

Today's Issues

Identify two major domestic policy issues and two foreign policy issues that America is facing. Using outside resources, briefly state the conservative and liberal positions on those issues and then state what you believe is the biblical position.

Issue	Conservative position	Liberal position	Biblical position
Domestic issue 1			
Domestic issue 2			
Foreign issue 1			
Foreign issue 2			

AMERICAN GOVERNMENT

CHAPTER 18 • ACTIVITY 2

Opinions About Public Opinion

Read the following quotations concerning public opinion from Presidents Jefferson and Van Buren. What does each say about public opinion? Do these observations hold true today? Support your answer.

Thomas Jefferson to Chevalier de Ouis, 1814

"An enlightened people, and an energetic **public opinion** . . . will control and enchain [bind, restrain] the aristocratic spirit of the government."

_____
_____
_____
_____
_____
_____
_____
_____
_____
_____

Thomas Jefferson to Lafayette, 1823

"The only security of all is in a free press. The force of **public opinion** cannot be resisted when permitted freely to be expressed. The agitation it produces must be submitted to. It is necessary, to keep the waters pure."

_____
_____
_____
_____
_____
_____
_____
_____
_____
_____

(continued on next page)

Martin Van Buren to the US Senate, 1826

"There is a power in **public opinion** in this country, and I thank God for it; for it is the most honest and best of all powers, which will not tolerate an incompetent or unworthy man to hold in his weak or wicked hands, the lives and fortunes of his fellow-citizens."

AMERICAN GOVERNMENT

Name _____

CHAPTER 18 • ACTIVITY 3

Contacting Public Officials

One way citizens can influence lawmakers is by contacting them to express an opinion. Identify a state or national issue that concerns you. Write a letter or an email to a state or national legislator about it. Be specific about your concerns and the outcome you desire. If the issue involves a bill that has been proposed, identify the bill. Ask for a direct response regarding the legislator's position.

Refer to page 458 of the textbook for more information about writing officials.

AMERICAN GOVERNMENT

Name _____

CHAPTER 18 • ACTIVITY 4

Mass Media Cartoon

Using a newspaper, a magazine, or the internet, find a political cartoon about an issue of interest to you. Place a copy of it in the space below. Answer the questions about the cartoon.

1. List the people/objects shown in the cartoon and explain what each represents. _____
   _____
   _____

2. What issue does the cartoon present? _____
   _____

3. What important words (if any) are used in the cartoon? What do those words indicate? _____
   _____
   _____

4. What message is the cartoonist communicating about this issue? What is his viewpoint? _____
   _____
   _____

AMERICAN GOVERNMENT

Name _____

CHAPTER 18 • ACTIVITY 5

Chapter Review

Answer the following questions.

1. Define *public policy*. _____
   _____

2. Define and give two characteristics of *public opinion*. _____
   _____
   _____
   _____

3. What word describes a philosophy that favors government action and supports government expansion?
   _____

4. What word describes a philosophy that is reluctant to expand government authority?
   _____

5. What word describes individuals who favor a middle-of-the-road political philosophy (between conservative and liberal)? _____

6. What issues are frequently included in domestic policy? _____
   _____

7. What issues are included in foreign policy? _____

8. Define *agenda*. _____

9. Identify important speeches in which the president outlines his agenda (though he does so at other times as well). _____

10. List six influences on public opinion. _____

11. List three ways public opinion is measured. _____
    _____

12. Define *opinion polls*. _____

13. Identify several ways a scientific poll attempts to obtain a representative sample of people. _____
    _____
    _____

(continued on next page)

14. What are straw polls? _____
    _____

15. Give another term for and define *interest groups*. _____
    _____

16. What is the largest labor organization in the United States? _____

17. What does the acronym NRA stand for? What does the organization do? _____
    _____

18. List five methods used by interest groups to influence public policy. _____
    _____

19. What is lobbying? _____

20. What are committees formed by interest groups to work on behalf of candidates whom they deem favorable to their goal? _____

21. What does the acronym ACLU stand for? What does this organization do? _____
    _____
    _____
    _____
    _____

22. What do the words *amicus curiae* mean, and to what does the phrase refer? _____
    _____

23. Define *mass media*. _____
    _____

24. Identify four US newspapers with large circulation. _____
    _____

25. What is C-SPAN, and what is one of its goals? _____
    _____
    _____
    _____

26. What is freedom from prior restraint? _____
    _____
    _____

(continued on next page)

27. Which law gives the media and private individuals broad powers to investigate files of the federal bureaucracy? _____

28. Define *shield laws*. _____
_____

29. What are the two limits to the media's freedom under the First Amendment? _____

30. What refers to published false statements that injure a person's reputation? _____

31. What is false oral communication that injures a person's reputation? _____

32. Which government agency can impose fines on radio stations for broadcasting obscene language or engaging in false advertising? _____

33. What is the term for using various techniques to select and manipulate information so as to persuade or influence people effectively? _____

163